They Never Saw Me I

TIMB

To
Bob Bratscher
with best wishes
of the Author,
Dick Timberlake

They Never Saw Me Then

Richard H. Timberlake Jr.

48-TIMB

Library of Congress Number: 2001119882
ISBN #: Hardcover 1-4010-4131-0
Softcover 1-4010-4130-2

This book was printed in the United States of America.

To order additional copies of this book, contact:
Xlibris Corporation
1-888-7-XLIBRIS
www.Xlibris.com
Orders@Xlibris.com

Contents

TO PATRICIA,

WHO WAS THERE

The author in London, late September 1944

Forewords

The U.S. Army's 8th Air Force suffered half of all Air Force casualties during the Second World War. During the 1,000 days that "The Mighty Eighth" was in action from bases in England, it lost nearly 5,000 aircraft and sustained more than 45,000 dead, missing, and wounded. The immensity of the contribution made by the men who flew the bombers and fighters on daylight missions deep into the heart of Germany cannot be exaggerated. Their terrible losses will forever be a reminder of the cost of war on humanity's most promising resource.

I was eleven years old when the Second World War began in 1939. It was difficult for me to comprehend the gravity of war or the implications of what was occurring. Indeed, the changes in my life were more exciting than threatening. I still attended school, though our classes were often held in air raid shelters. On warm summer afternoons, the sound of distant machine-gun fire often interrupted our cricket games. When we looked up, we would see the condensation trails of hostile and friendly aircraft fighting the Battle of Britain high overhead. At night, when the German bombers flew toward London, I would sleep soundly in our garden air-raid shelter whilst anti-aircraft guns boomed nearby and bombs fell.

As time passed, I joined the local Squadron of the Air Training Corps. We were taught aircraft recognition, how to navigate, and to "fly" the Link Trainer. I prayed that the war would last long enough for me to sit at the controls of a Spitfire and join the battle. Often I would travel to London in my Training Corps uniform and board a bus that would take me to the U.S. Air Force base at Bovington. There I was allowed to eat in the Transit Mess, where wonderfully exotic food would be served: fried chicken, sweet corn, grapefruit—endless delights for a hungry lad. While in the mess, I was at times able to persuade cigar-smoking 8th Air Force pilots to take me on aircraft test or communication flights. These men were my heroes. With them, I flew in the B-17 Flying Fortress, and the B-24 Liberator. Sometimes, I found myself far from home. These excursions caused my parents great anxiety, and had me miss school for a few days. But I didn't care. Life was exciting, and I was tasting much of it.

It was about this time that my elder sister, Patricia, introduced the Author of this book to our family. I have a recollection, clouded by years, of a tall, young, dark-haired officer with the silver wings of a pilot on his dark green uniform. I remember being spellbound by the knowledge that he was a bomber pilot. None of us fully appreciated the daily risks that he endured flying his B-17 on those daylight raids against the enemy, until we learned that he had been wounded by flak and repatriated to the United States.

Richard Timberlake's record is a vivid reminder of the horrors of war, and a poignant testimony to the bravery of the men who fought in it. I salute them.

David G. Hart

Rosemarkie, Fortrose, Scotland

March 2001

Almost at the eleventh hour, Richard Timberlake decided that he must tell his story. The pages following, describing 'the way it was' 56 years ago, do so though his eyes and his memories.

Who amongst the men in the U.S. Eighth Air Force's 388th Bomb Group of that time—1944—could have hoped to survive long enough to witness the new century? Anyone perusing this account of aerial episodes in that era will understand how precious just one more day was when the B-17's wheels touched down on Knettishall's runways. It was that bit of England that welcomed the bomber crews back, and England became 'home' to everyone serving in the Eighth Air Force.

In this observer's opinion, Richard has covered every aspect of how an airman's flying experiences relentlessly unfolded day after day. Ultimately, he became a victim of flak wounds and received a ticket back to the United States.

At this time (1944-1945) I was a fourteen-year-old English Air Cadet. My home's proximity to the Knettishall Air Base provided me the opportunity to mix freely with many 388th Bomb Group personnel. Sometimes, their conversation turned to the question of whether infantry soldiers or bomber crews had it 'rougher.' The airmen's observation was: "There aren't any foxholes at twenty-five thousand feet." They also noted that the Alclad aluminum skin of a B-17 was no defense against flak or the 20-mm. cannon fire from a Messerschmidt 109.

I was allowed to accompany some few crews on practice mission flights in these B-17s, but never did I witness the terror those men felt for the next mission they would fly. Readers of this book will discover for themselves why and how such feelings must have arisen. They will understand even better if they visit the American cemetery in Cambridge. The graves of the young men buried there are witness to what happened. Richard Timberlake's, They Never Saw Me Then, records much of what they endured.

George Stebbings

Rickinghall, Diss,
Norfolk, March 2001

Preface

This little book focuses on my flying experiences during World War II. It covers primarily the period from February 1943 to April 1945. At the beginning I explain why and how I got into the Army Air Corps (as it was then labeled) and at the end I include an account of my partial convalescence in a U.S. Army hospital in England. Otherwise, I stick closely to my actual flying experiences and the events of that era. I omit all but a trivial amount of personal experiences outside of flying.

I have compiled this account from several sources: (1) my memory and my official flight record; (2) the letters I wrote to my immediate family while I was in the Air Corps, which I repossessed after my parents died; (3) official Eighth Air Force records of bombing missions; (4) accounts written by former crew members, Larry Locker, John R. Wingfield, and Fred Stoker; and (5) the book, The 388th at War, by Edward Huntzinger. During the war, I had a diary in which I kept brief accounts of day-to-day events. However, some eager lackey, who must have known that diaries were officially forbidden, removed it from my belongings in March 1945 when he transferred them from my bomber unit to the Army hospital where I was convalescing. Fortunately, I could verify the dates and events that I include in this account by means of these other sources.

Long ago, I determined to write this chronicle if I survived my combat tour. I felt that it would be the least I could do for those who will never grow old and can never speak for themselves. I do not pretend to speak for them. Nevertheless, if my account is only one among many that bears witness to the trauma and agony of politically organized human conflict, it will have served its purpose.

The title I have chosen derives from the common thought many of us have when we are suddenly enveloped in Big Events, such as, for example, World War II. "Boy, if they could see me now," we think, as we imagine all the people—family, friends, and "enemies"—who might gasp in awe and admiration at our exploits. But . . . They Never Saw Me Then. Since "they" did not see me then, my only recourse is to tell the story myself.

I was a young man—a boy, really, 21-22 years old—during 1943 and 1944. I was one among millions of young men fighting millions of other young men, all of whom might have been friends if not for the circumstances of time and place in which they happened to live. Arthur Hoppe, a journalist for The San Francisco Chronicle, had it right. In a column on "The Meaning of War," he wrote:

> "I think most men in combat are trapped by fear—fear of their officers, fear of the opinions of their fellow soldiers, and fear of military prison and disgrace if they turn and run. So, trapped by fear, they attack the enemy. . . .
>
> I suppose there were a few in World War II who were fighting for freedom or democracy, but in my three years in the Navy I never met one of them. . . .
>
> [W]e were fighting to stay alive. And that is the true horror of war.
>
> *San Francisco Chronicle,* 5 August 1998.

My experience in World War II substantiates Hoppe's observation. All my fellow airmen and I knew that Hitler and his henchmen were atrocious and loathsome examples of the human race. Yet, any U.S. soldier or airman, who thought even briefly about his job of trying to kill and destroy "the enemy," knew that he was not within range of damaging Hitler and other Nazi leaders. We could not reach their personal environments or influence their decisions; our activities were many magnitudes removed from hurting them. We could only chip away at the peripheries of their domain and hope that they would realize the futility and fallacy of their ways. To do so, we had to try and kill our enemy counterparts with whom we had no personal quarrel at all. We aimed our bombs at their strategic war-making industries and infrastructure, but in the process we knew we could not avoid hitting churches, schools, and innocent people. Many of us thought that a better way must exist. Fifty-six years later, I still think so.

The strategy that I think would work best begins

with everyone letting everyone else alone to do as he sees fit—laissez faire—within a framework of easily understood and commonly accepted rules of behavior. It ends with governments, in their domestic role, staying rigorously within their constitutional boundaries of protecting individuals from force and fraud. Finally, in their external affairs governments must resist any temptation to intervene in the affairs of other peoples. It takes a government to wage a war. So governments must take the same oath of nonintervention—live-and-let-live—with other governments as each individual observes with other individuals. The model for this point-of-view is the political system the Founding Fathers put together when they wrote The Constitution of the United States.

The twentieth century witnessed two horrible world wars and dozens of lesser conflicts. Surely, if societies owe anything to the veterans of former wars and the innocent soldiers and people destroyed in those catastrophes, it is a responsibility to avoid further warfare by every practicable means. So far as I can see from my present vantagepoint, societies and governments are not following my simple prescription—or any other effective strategy—for preventing wars of all varieties. In not doing so, they are betraying the trust that my wartime colleagues, especially those who made the ultimate sacrifice, and I reposed in them.

Chapter 1: The Nature of War and How It Got to Me

War is the mutual destruction of capital, both human and nonhuman. To achieve capital destruction of their enemies, the antagonists must use up their own capital. A common term for this action and reaction is, *attrition,* the single word that best describes what war is all about no matter what its causes.

The demands of virtually any war permit governments to throw away constitutional restraints on expansionary monetary and fiscal policies so that military agencies may indulge their insatiable appetites for resources to fight the war. Government central banks and treasuries pump new money into all the channels that furnish military services, and this stimulus quickly overwhelms any recession or depression that happens to be around. War itself has no positive economic impact on business doldrums. The stimulus comes from the burgeoning supplies of paper money and expanded bank reserves. The new money would have the same effect whether a war was around or not.

Contrary to most popular belief, the necessities of war also depress most technological innovations and inventions. Some new technology, such as radar and the development of nuclear technology during World War II, may seem to contradict this observation. One has only to look at extended periods of war, however, and compare them with extended periods of peace to see that the large bulk of innovative technology occurs during peacetime. Only in an unregimented environment, in which free minds can work unconstrained and test their products in free markets, can enduring technological progress occur. Wartime "advances" are largely results of technology developed during peacetime and accelerated into operational use once hostilities begin. Sheer quantities of men and armaments are the stuff of war.

I did not think along such lines in 1941and 1942 when I was caught up in the popular "necessity" and enthusiasm for World War II. On Pearl Harbor Day 7 December 1941, I was trying to think of something sensible to say to the mother of a current girl friend, just after we had heard the shocking news of the Japanese attack on Pearl Harbor. I recalled all the stories of the wasted resources of the 1930s—the years of the Great Depression, when six million little pigs were killed, thousands of gallons of milk dumped on the ground, and large quantities of agricultural products stored in caves in Kentucky, all as a part of the federal government's policy to "raise prices."

"Well," I remarked, "at least the war will stop all this waste." Whereupon the lady gently corrected me. "Dick," she said, "all war is waste." She was only too right.

I had been interested in flying since my early teens. During those years, 1934-1940, I built dozens of flying model airplanes made primarily of balsa wood and tissue paper. "Megow" was the favorite brand of model builders then. I also read all the books I could find on the experiences of prominent airmen, many of whom had flown during World War I. I devoured aeronautical pulp fiction and as much scientific information about aircraft and weather as I could absorb. I also managed to take two legitimate courses in aeronautics and meteorology when I was a junior in college in 1941-42. So, as the time for my mandatory military service approached in 1942, I enlisted in the United States Army Air Corps with the self-righteous feeling that I would probably have done so anyway. I managed to do well on the Air Corps qualifying exam, and was sworn in as a reservist in October 1942 while I was in my senior year of college.

The reserve status did not last long. In February 1943, the military authorities called me, along with thousands of other reservists, to active duty, just a few months before I would have graduated from college. I reported for induction at Fort Campbell, Kentucky, on 19 February 1943, and was put on a troop train the next day with hundreds of other inductees. Our destination was Keesler Field, Mississippi, where we were to undergo basic training. The train ride took the better part of two days. It was a

8-TIMB

boring and uncomfortable journey, interrupted by long waits on railroad sidings as our train was fit into the railroad's busy transportation schedule. I was at Keesler Field for twelve days during which time I took many tests, learned how to march and drill, and received inoculations against disease and infection. No aircraft were anywhere in sight. Then it was another troop train for a trip back north.

Troop trains were always sit-up-all-night coaches. They had been built in an earlier era—pre-World War I, when passenger traffic might have provided the railroads with some revenues. One slept sitting up in them or one did not sleep. Most of us managed a sort of numbing compromise between these two states. For meals we went to the "dining" car, which was simply an open kitchen. We lined up through the coaches with our steel mess kits and received our portions of Army food. The food was passable, but the cars had poor and inadequate sanitary facilities. The impossibility of getting even a minimal amount of sleep was their worst feature. In addition, due to the heavy wartime traffic, it took them forever to get where they were going.

After three days on this train, we arrived at Carlisle, Pennsylvania, where we began attending classes at Dickinson College as part of the Army Air Corps's College Training Detachment (CTD). This program was supposed to give budding airmen college level courses in math and physics so they would be better equipped to fly, or fly in, military aircraft. Official Army orders designated us as "aircrew students" rather than "aviation cadets," the label we all had expected. Our pay was $50 per month, the same amount paid to privates in any branch of the U.S. Army, rather than the $75 per month paid to aviation cadets. Consequently, we labeled ourselves "air screwed students."

I was one of the more "advanced" students. Only two weeks earlier I had been a college senior, majoring in physics and mathematics, and almost ready to graduate. Now I was back in college taking elementary math and physics courses that I had been through three years earlier. The phrase had not yet been coined, but it was clearly a case of, "One size fits all." Individual differences meant nothing; everyone had to fit into "the program."

Our living quarters at Dickinson were the dormitories in which Dickinson's men students had roomed. Most of those students had been drafted or had enlisted in some branch of the military. So the repopulation of the campus with aircrew students simply filled in the gaps left by the forced departure of former male students. We also took the classes they might have taken, and thereby kept the faculty busy. Most of the former students were undoubtedly in other specialized college training programs at other colleges or universities. It all seemed like an enlarged "musical chairs" operation.

We had increased the number of male students by a factor of about '3' over what that number had been. The dormitory I occupied, Denny Hall, had housed about 150 students. Now it had 400-plus "airscrewed" students. Where normally, students were two or three to a room, they now were six or eight. Two Army bunk beds often replaced a single ordinary bed—that is, four bodies in place of one body, but such facile multiples could not work in bathrooms and some other places. I can never remember taking a comfortable hot shower in my six weeks at Dickinson. The hot water was always used up. We were lucky if it was just lukewarm.

All the new aircrew students had taken a uniform comprehensive mathematics-physics examination while in basic training a few weeks earlier. We now learned that the purpose of that exam was to decide our tenure in the college training program—that is, how long we would stay at Dickinson before moving on to the cadet classification center at Nashville, Tennessee.

Early one morning we all crowded into the main hallway of Denny Hall for our usual briefing on the day's special orders and requirements. The student "colonel" in charge then read off each student's name and the score he had received on the qualifying exam. Much to my puzzlement, the student leader did not call out my name and score. I wondered if I had missed something. So, as the crowd broke up, I pushed forward to the "colonel" and asked him why my name was missing. He replied that my score was special because my grade on the exam was the highest of all the airscrewed students at Dickinson!

I was shocked. Somehow it was too early in the morning for me to grasp the fact that I had done anything extraordinary. On the other hand, only a month earlier I had been taking advanced courses in the main subjects on the exam, so I should have done well. My score was 117 out of a possible 150. It was the only military exam that I can remember that had some really tough analytical questions on it.

Because of my grade on this exam, I was in the first group to leave the college training detachment. On 15 April 1943, a troop train transported about 75 of us to the Army Air Corps Classification Center in Nashville, Tennessee. There, after extensive testing, I duly qualified physically and mentally as an aviation cadet eligible for pilot training.

The tests were for both mental and physical abilities, especially hand-eye coordination. All these examinations came under the rubric of 'Adaptability Rating for Military Aeronautics' (ARMA). Near the end of the exam, a psychologist interviewed each of us to see if we had the right attitude and stomach for this new calling. One of the questions my interrogator asked me was whether I had ever thought about the possibility that I might get shot down and killed in the line of duty. I remember only too well my shallow and immature answer.

"Yes, sir, I have thought about the possibility" I replied.

"And," he next asked, "how do you regard this possibility?"

"Well." I said smugly, "it's a quick way to die[!]"

Oh you fool; you will live to rue such fatuous sophistry! Yes, I will. But should I, not yet twenty-one, have had the wisdom of the ages to give a suitably profound and humble answer to this question?

Chapter 2: Pre-Flight

In late May 1943, another military troop train transported hundreds of other eager would-be pilots and me to Maxwell Field, Alabama, for the preflight phase of pilot training. Once in preflight training, we became full-fledged cadets. Since the four phases of flight training—pre-flight, primary, basic, and advanced—were to take two months each, our class was scheduled to graduate in February 1944. We, therefore, were in the pilot class of 44-B. Most of us in 44-B were initially aircrew students who had qualified to leave in the first group from a CTD. Consequently, I claim foolishly and vainly—perhaps, in vain—that we were the "best pilot class that ever came through the U.S. Army Air Corps." I know, I know, everyone thinks his was the best. I simply reflect "everyone."

The two-month ordeal at Maxwell Field during June and July of 1943 was certainly the most uncomfortable and unpleasant time of my short life. Since I had just turned twenty-one in June, I had not lived long enough to know how bad things could be, especially at an army base, during a war, and in the deep South in the summer.

Preflight was the Army Air Corps's short-term substitute for military school training programs at West Point, Annapolis, Quantico, or what have you. While the burdens of preflight at Maxwell were torturous and exhausting, they were not nearly as rigorous and demanding as the more established military schools. Rather, Maxwell was an expedient wartime surrogate to train men quickly. Our ordeal lasted only two months, and the worst of it was the one-month period during which we were "underclassmen."

The two scorching months at Maxwell were a dreary round of marches, drills, physical training, and harassment from our upper class tormentors. We sat in non-air-conditioned military classrooms learning material germane to our existence as soldiers and airmen: meteorology, weapons, aircraft identification, the workings of internal combustion engines, principles of flight, and Morse code. However, we never saw a plane, either on the ground or in the air.

We lived in two-story wooden barracks that had no interior walls. Two-by-four studs separated the "rooms," but no wall material of any kind was fastened to the studs. So we could talk to our fellow cadets in other rooms without hindrance. Each room contained three or four cadets with all their clothes and equipment. Plasterboard walls, however, did enclose latrines and the rooms of cadet officers.

Numerous Air Corps tactical officers—"tac officers"—regimented and structured all our activities so that we would learn to do things the Army way. Sweat—how to treat it, and cockroaches—how to avoid them, were the most memorable features of our tenure at Maxwell. No, we could not avoid the sweat and sunburn; and, no, we could not treat the cockroaches in any meaningful way.

During the second month at Maxwell when we were "upperclassmen," military authority granted us "open post" on Saturday nights. However, this brief freedom was difficult to exploit in any satisfactory manner. All that a cadet saw when he was outside the confines of the military base were other khaki-clad cadets.

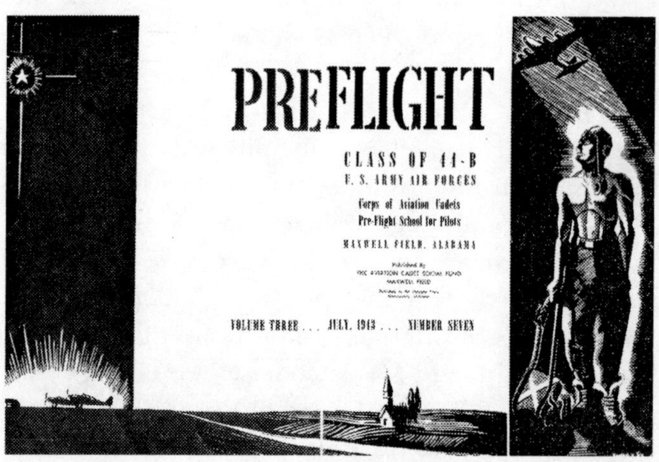

Title page from booklet, PREFLIGHT, Class of 44-B

Large formations of cadets were the mainstay of life at Maxwell. Several evenings each week, we formed into our specific groups and squadrons, and marched to the big parade ground. There, we endured "Retreat," and passed in review before the commanding officer and his staff while the brass band played the "Air Corps Song"—"Off We Go, etc." We then marched back to our barracks for dismissal, supper, letter writing, and sleep.

Our first "Open Post," came on our fourth Saturday at Maxwell. It extended for many cadets into Sunday, since Sundays were also a part of Open Post—until 1700 hours. However, by five o'clock on Sunday afternoon, we were officially on duty again. To reorient us, in case we had forgotten what Maxwell was like, we always had a "Retreat" ceremony, and a pass-in-review formation to attend at this hour on Sunday.

The release that the first Open Post provided from the stiff-necked training we were getting was too much for several of my fellow cadets. Even as late as five o'clock on that first open-post Sunday, many of them were still on very shaky ground—still in Hangover County. Nonetheless, we all formed into the required formation to march to "Retreat." Of course, the weather was hot and humid; it was never anything else.

During the flag-lowering ceremony at the parade ground, we were required to stand at stiff attention. Since I was relatively tall and therefore near the front ranks of cadets, I could not see what was going on in back. As the ceremony progressed, however, I thought I heard an unusual 'thump' behind me, then another, and a few more.

What I heard was bodies hitting the ground. My colleagues who had partied too much and for too long were passing out from the heat, tension, and locked knees. After the flag was lowered and we swung around to pass in review, I saw the half a dozen or so who had "gone down," sitting on the grass and trying to regain their bearings. Their lot was not pleasant to contemplate, for by their behavior they had proven derelict in their duties and could expect no charity from a penalty board.

Very often during my stay at Maxwell Field, although I never abused "Open Post," I was guilty of minor infractions that resulted in demerits and disciplinary penalties. Given my enduring penchant not to be regimented, this result was inevitable—though I often kicked myself for not going along with the collectivist rules to avoid punishments.

The principal penalty for these minor infractions was walking tours Saturday nights and Sunday mornings when I might otherwise have been free for a few hours. Walking a short closed course repetitively in south Alabama in the summer is tedious and boring beyond description. It could have been worse: Like Sisyphus, I could also have been rolling a stone up a hill, or, the Army equivalent, digging a ditch and filling it in again.

To add insult to injury, I had tours to walk off even as we came to the end of our tenure at Maxwell. However, I was alert enough to notice that whoever did the accounting of such things had miscalculated my tour penalty. So I respectfully reported this error to the tac officer in charge of our squadron. He checked on the matter, and found I was correct that the penalty calculator had made an error. He acknowledged that I had been over-penalized by twelve hours of tours. Nevertheless, he concluded in true Army fashion, that since official reports had already codified the error, I would just have to walk off the undeserved tours! So it was, I learned, that even if one were right in the Army he could still be "wrong."

Fortunately, the official flight-training program called for my cadet class to report to a primary flight training field two days hence. By the time we were scheduled to depart, I had walked off only three or four of the undeserved tours. Nonetheless, the squadron tac officer, who had approved the incorrect tour tally (and whose name was Zimaldi), threatened that I might have to stay another month at Maxwell to complete my "punishment." Fortunately, the authorities in charge of cadet logistics did not countenance this possibility, due probably to the perceived need for pilots. So when my cadet class packed up and boarded the train for primary flight training, I was with them.

Thank goodness! I look back on my Maxwell Field experience with loathing. So far as I can recall, it did nothing for me except to reinforce my distaste for authoritarianism. I certainly did not have the "right attitude" about that form of social organization.

Chapter 3: Primary Flight Training

On 28 July 1943, a train ride of several hours took us—perhaps 300 hundred cadets—from Maxwell Field to our primary flight training base, Darr Aero Tech, some five miles west of Albany, Georgia. Though it was well after dark when we arrived, the commanding officer at Darr had the mess hall personnel serve us cold fried chicken! He also welcomed us with a speech that seemed to imply a world of difference between Darr Aero Tech and what we had endured at Maxwell Field. I was one happy cadet when I went to bed that night.

Our quarters at Darr were two-story barracks, but significantly more comfortable than what we had at Maxwell. I was on a second floor along with dozens of other aspiring pilots. Each of us had a bunk, clothes locker, and dresser for our personal belongings. Again, no partitions separated us one from another.

If a cadet folded his trousers over a hanger preparing to hang them in his locker, everyone in the building could hear his coins tumble out when he forgot first to empty his pockets of change. However, the barracks were comfortable, and most of the cockroaches were still in Alabama.

The Stearman PT-17 primary trainer

The plane we flew in primary flight training was the Stearman PT-17 biplane, an aircraft that has become a classic. It had a 220-horsepower Continental engine with a fixed-pitch wooden propeller and fixed landing gear. The two wings were virtually identical surfaces. Short struts out of the upper fuselage and the old fashioned 'N' struts between wings braced the wings. Guy wires also crisscrossed between wings and fuselage to strengthen them further. All the covering on the plane was treated fabric.

The PT-17 had two cockpits in tandem. The instructor sat in the front seat, which was slightly elevated when the plane was on the ground. His position gave him an excellent view of the world so that he could keep the student and himself out of trouble. Rudder pedals steered the tail wheel while the plane was on the ground and provided directional flying control once the plane was airborne. A real wooden stick in each cockpit controlled the wing ailerons for bank-and turn, and the elevators on the tail stabilizer for ascent and descent.

With the instructor and student in their respective places ready for flight, another student cranked the flywheel to get the engine started. The adjunct cadet would stand on the lower left wing near the fuselage and grasp a crank handle in the nacelle just behind the engine compartment. Turning this crank activated a heavy flywheel. As the flywheel built up speed, it gave off an exciting whine that became higher and higher pitched. When the pilot judged that the flywheel had enough rotational momentum, he shouted, "Contact," and simultaneously switched on the magnetos to provide ignition. The student-assistant replied, "Contact," and pulled a ring attached to a short cable on the engine cowling that caused the flywheel to engage the engine's crankshaft through an internal clutch. Meshing gears interrupted the flywheel's high-pitched scream as they transferred its rotational energy to the inert crankshaft of the engine. As the engine started turning, it sucked gas and air into the cylinders already primed with fuel to which the magnetos then provided a high-voltage spark. The engine coughed into life, then gradually smoothed out until it was running properly. The cadet assistant, his role completed, stowed the crank handle in its receptacle, backed off the wing and departed. Meanwhile, the instructor and student waited for the engine to warm up.

The instructor talked to his cadet student through what was called a Gosport tube, a device that featured a mouthpiece attached to plastic or rubber tubes running back to receivers connected to the student's helmet. It was strictly one-way; no analogous device allowed the student to initiate a question or a response. His only means of answering was to shake his head up and down, or sideways. The instructor could see these answers in the rear view mirror mounted on the cowl beside his cockpit. Sometimes, a student-pilot might shout something above the roar of the engine, but most discussion from student to instructor could only occur before the flight began or after it had ended.

Primary instructors were all civilians, but had the status of Army officers. Mr. Soldano, my first primary instructor, was an excellent teacher. Our first ride together in early August 1943, and my first ride ever in an airplane, was uneventful. However, I could tell right away that operating in this new medium was going to be a challenge. I was adept at driving a car. However, a car had only two dimensions of movement in which its driver could go wrong, a plane had three.

On the second ride the next day, Mr. Soldano showed me turns. First, we did a shallow turn with the tip of the upper wing just touching the horizon; then a medium turn, about 45°, with the wings banked so that the strut wires between the wings on one side of the plane were level with the horizon. Finally he showed me a steep turn, with the wings banked over about eighty degrees from the horizontal, and the control stick pulled back tight to keep the plane at its given altitude. At this angle, one of the short struts between the upper wing and the engine nacelle was level with the horizon.

This maneuver, with its attendant G-forces and whirling scenery, was too much for my fragile stomach. I thereupon popped my cookies back over the fuselage and tail assembly. If for no other reason, this typical student reaction to unfamiliar motion was a sufficient cause for the instructor to sit in the front seat. Upon landing, I ingloriously gathered together a scrub bucket, laundry soap, and a cleaning brush and washed down the fuselage behind the rear cockpit. Cadets knew this experience as: "Joining the bucket brigade," and many of my cadet friends were members of this "club." It was an especially acute problem if one was scheduled to fly in the early afternoon, because the hot sun burbled the lower air levels with thermals as the day progressed. We learned to be very careful of what wc atc for lunch.

I wish I could say that I took to flying like a hawk, and as I expected to, but I was not that gifted. I inferred intuitively that the difficulty of maneuvering any vehicle increased by the square of the dimensions in which it operated. That untestable hypothesis being true, flying an airplane would be more than twice as difficult as driving a car. Other factors made the experience even more exacting. We wore uncomfortable parachutes, which also served as seat cushions in the cockpit. We had to navigate conscientiously, and keep constant track of weather conditions. Finally, the plane itself was very sensitive to its control mechanisms, although it was also very slow.

All the struts, wires, and fixed landing gear offered so much air resistance that a Stearman in good condition would hardly get above 100 miles per hour (mph), even though its rated top speed was 125 mph. However, it would turn on the proverbial dime, and it performed all the usual aerobatics most eagerly. To make it land a little "hotter," aeronautical engineers had fixed a triangular strip of wood along the leading edge of the lower wing. This device acted as a "spoiler" to the airflow over the lower wing so that the plane would stall out at a higher speed. Thus, its landing speed was higher than it otherwise would have been. Conventional aircraft stall out to land, which is why we student-pilots practiced stalls and their recovery so rigorously before soloing.

The touchdown speed for a three-point landing was about 55 mph. While that is not dreadfully fast, the plane's narrow landing gear added to the excitement. A student-pilot had to be very alert that he had the Stearman's directional axis aligned with the runway. For at touchdown the plane's flight in three dimensions suddenly changed to a steering operation in two dimensions. With only a tail wheel to steer it and the too-narrowly-spaced front wheels not able to provide needed lateral stability, a PT-17 improperly aligned could suddenly veer to one side or the other, then spin around in a cloud of dust before coming to a stop. Cadet custom labeled this unhappy maneuver a "ground loop." Students who suffered through such an embarrassment were required to wear the insignia wings on their garrison caps at a forty-five-degree angle. Sometimes, the plane in a ground loop would sustain minor scrapes to the wings, but it was rarely a life-threatening event.

After I had about four or five hours of instruction, I knew I was not progressing well enough. Landing the plane was the big obstacle for everyone, including me. If one could not land the plane safely, he could not solo. If he could not solo, it was, "Bye-bye, baby. See you in navigators' (or bombardiers') school." My landings were bumpy and uncertain. Furthermore, I could not summon up any confidence in the whole activity of flying. In desperation, when I had an hour off, I went out by myself to the flight line and climbed into an idle plane to practice 'dry flying.'

A cadet friend of mine had suggested to some of my fellow cadets and me a very useful gimmick for making one-bounce-and-stay-down landings—a method that an instructor had relayed to him. On the approach to the landing, the advisory went, keep telling yourself to get the stick back, Back, **Back**, until it is in your gut, and the plane is completely stalled out. This method meant total commitment to the landing, but it also meant that the plane would land and stay landed. For if the wings are completely stalled out, they have no lift left to take the plane off again for even a brief period. No lift meant no grasshopper bounces, and no struggling for control in the nether region between flying in the air and taxiing on the ground.

I immersed myself in the environment of the

grounded PT-17 on these dry runs. back, Back, **Back** I brought the control stick in these landing pantomimes. Besides improving my mechanics for landing, I became more familiar with all the details of the cockpit so that I did not have to think about them when actually flying.

On my own I had discovered a crude form of what is today called a *simulator*. My "simulator" was nothing more complicated than the plane itself, on the ground, inert, and with no instructor except myself to put me through the required exercises. Well, it seemed to work. I finally began to feel familiar with the aircraft—as if I belonged in it. However, I had yet to prove that my new sense of confidence was well founded for I had not soloed.

During my sixth hour of instruction, the benefits of my extracurricular activity began to bear real fruit. My flying procedures became more regular and my landings began to stay put.

Then on my seventh hour, really good things happened. Mr. Soldano had us at a practice field—a grassy strip with no facilities or personnel, and only a windsock to show wind direction. Several such fields were found in areas a few miles from the main field to provide landing practice. I was flying the Stearman, and on the final approach to the first landing, I did everything just right. The stick was all the way back in my gut when the wheels touched, and my landing was letter perfect.

The instructor then pushed the throttle full forward, and told me to take off without coming to a complete stop—a so-called touch-and-go. We came around for another approach, and again I made a perfect landing. And again.

After the fourth or fifth landing, and as we were

taxiing, I noticed him shaking his head side-to-side, *not* up-and-down. "What's wrong?" I asked above the idling engine noise, fearing I might have overlooked some detail of landing procedure. "Nothing," he replied. "*They're too good* [sic]."

Too good! What the hell is this? How can my landings be "too good?" Are they "too good" just because Cadet Timberlake made them, and he isn't good enough to do that? Is this "logic" more realistic than the fact that he was the one who actually made the landings?

Before I could analyze his remark any further, he told me to take off again and return to the main field. His order seemed to imply that his opinion of my landings was just what I had inferred. Very disappointed, I did as he ordered. As I rounded out my approach for the landing at the main field, he suddenly wrenched the stick out of my hand and landed the plane himself. "There, you see," he exclaimed. "You were not properly lined up. You would have ground-looped."

I do not believe that my last approach had been faulty. Nevertheless, even if I had mistimed the landing or made some other procedural error, it was because of the consternation his remark had caused me. I knew that I had been ready to solo, but that my alleged glitch on this last landing had set me back a significant step. I was very discouraged. What good is it to achieve through one's own initiative and extra work when the authority in judgment simply will not believe the evidence? In not giving me credit where credit was due, the instructor presumed I was not ready to solo. He practically made his inference a self-fulfilling prophecy.

Still, life had to go on. So I continued to concentrate on further improving my techniques; I had no recourse but to keep trying. Fortunately, after a few more hours of formal instruction I soloed on 20 August 1943. I had 11 hours of flying time when Mr. Soldano finally let me do it alone. Happy as I was to have achieved solo status, it was largely anticlimactic; I knew I had been ready four flying hours earlier. However, I had too much ahead of me to dwell further on this disappointing experience.

161 Lbs. Height 6 Ft. 1½

nature of Issuing Officer:

ERRITT N. WILLITS

Issued

Aviation cadet I.D. of the author, August 1943

Primary flight training was interesting and often much fun. Many obstacles still lay ahead, however, the first being the twenty-hour check ride. For this test, a special check-pilot flew with the student. His job was to ensure that by the twenty-hour point the student's progress on the procedures and mechanics of flying had reached an acceptable level. It was a dreaded ordeal and washed out a sizable fraction of cadets. However, I did not have any real problems either with this test or with the 40-hour check ride that came some weeks later.

The author in Albany, Georgia, September 1943

Since I had soloed, I could go out by myself and practice the procedures I had learned. Instruction in acrobatics continued in parallel to our solo flights. On my own one day, I figured out how to do a loop: Climb to a safe altitude, and put the plane in a dive to get up enough speed. Then, put back-pressure on the stick to force the plane up and over itself to complete the maneuver. It seemed elementary, and when I tried it on my own, it was. Of course, I did not let on anything a few days later when my instructor "taught" it to me. He showed me how, and then I did it perfectly. Oh, but I was a wise guy—remember, all of 21 years old.

I also indulged in a little extracurricular activity—dogfighting, which was strictly forbidden. Some other misdemeanors were forgivable, but dogfighting was a capital offense punishable by expulsion from the program. Nonetheless, the Y-chromosome being what it is, some of us were bound to try it, and some of us were bound to get caught. Those of us with adventurous dispositions simply could not avoid temptation.

So it was that a friend of mine and I, when we saw each other going out to the flight line for solo practice one day, schemed to meet in the air near Sasser, Georgia, a small town northwest of Albany. We agreed that we would waggle wings a certain number of times for identification when either of us saw the other, then have at you!

Well, everything worked out as we planned. We were supposed to practice acrobatics anyway, so we flew to the designated area by different routes, identified each other with our wing-waggle, and began our little mischief. We were World War I pilots in our Spads. (Or were they S.E.5s, or Sopwith Camels?

Indeed, the Stearman was very much like a World War I fighter plane.) No matter. Have at you Nicholas, my "enemy!" Around we went, and up and down, and with plenty of acrobatics. Then, overcome with the exhilaration of the activity, we went down to a very low altitude and came in over Sasser as if strafing an enemy stronghold. Sasser's water tower was the only structure to be avoided, and we did so simply by pumping it full of make-believe machine-gun slugs, then pulling up over it! Oh, but we were "hot."

Eventually we had enough, returned to the main field from different directions and landed. Naturally, we related our adventures to our colleagues with much glee and some exaggeration. We should have been more discreet for our own good if nothing else, but I was one-and-twenty and had not yet listened to a wise man.

Having been successful once, we had to try it again a week or so later. Of course, we were apprehended. Fortunately, when caught we were not doing any 'advanced' dogfighting. We had made a trivial pass or two at each other, and we were practicing acrobatics, although not quite in the approved manner.

Another Stearman suddenly appeared out of nowhere. It obviously had an instructor in the front seat, and he could read our planes' numbers only too easily. When we got back to the field, our instructors were waiting for us. They "dressed us down good," then gave us the ultimatum: Do that again and you are out—spelled O-U-T. No words in their discourse required a dictionary or any further explanation.

This experience cured us of any more dogfighting. We did not realize how vulnerable to fatal miscues we were, and how quickly our inexperience could translate into disaster. I look back on that incident now with anything but pride. We had not grown up; we were not accomplished flyboys, and we had much more to learn than we realized.

By the time primary flight training ended, I had about 65 hours flying time. For all cadets the last ride in primary was in the front cockpit. The instructors put up with this custom, but they also cut it short, so we did not get to revel much in our achievement. Nonetheless, it was a big step forward and we were on our way.

Chapter 4: Basic Flight Training

On 28 September 1943 our cadet class left Darr Aero Tech on another troop train. Our destination was Greenwood Army Air Base near Greenwood, Mississippi, for the second phase of flight training called "Basic." Our quarters at the Greenwood Base were apartment style wooden barracks. Each apartment consisted of two small bedrooms with a common living room. The living room had tables for studying and writing. Four to six cadets occupied each apartment. This set-up, although Spartan and rough in many respects, was by far the most comfortable and enjoyable living arrangement I experienced as a cadet. By contrast, the food at Greenwood was certainly the worst any of us had yet endured.

The plane we were to fly was the Vultee BT-13, a low-wing monoplane with fixed landing gear and a 450-horsepower Pratt&Whitney radial engine. It also had a two-pitch propeller. "Low pitch" angled the propeller so that its "bite" was shallow relative to the forward motion of the plane. Similar to "low" gear in an automobile, this prop setting provided faster acceleration for take-off and more positive control for landing. "High pitch" was used for ordinary cruising speeds at altitude and just about everything else. The wooden propeller of the Stearman we had flown in primary had only one pitch that had to be relatively flat so that the plane could take-off and land safely. This constraint severely limited its top speed.

As the pilot revved up the BT-13's engine in flat pitch to take off, the propeller tips approached sonic speed and consequently emitted an unpleasant "blatting" roar. After take-off and the ascent to the desired altitude, the pilot appropriately changed the prop angle—shifted gears—to high pitch. Engine revolutions (rpms) and the prop speed then dropped off, and a more tolerable sound replaced the indigestible blatting.

Cadets sat in the front cockpit of the BT-13 from the beginning of instruction. The BT-13 also had a Plexiglas canopy over both cockpits. In addition, we had radio communication, not only between the instructor and student-pilot but also between the plane and the control tower at the main field.

To start the BT's engine, the pilot first primed the engine's cylinders by pushing a plunger that injected gas into them. Next, he turned to a two-position toggle switch near the dash panel labeled "Energize" and "Engage." When he pushed the switch to "Energize," the plane's battery started the flywheel motor turning, which then built up to the same dramatic high-pitched whine as the one in the PT-17. As the flywheel reached sufficient speed, the pilot toggled the switch to "Engage," and switched on the magnetos. As in the PT-17, the flywheel's scream would turn into a tortured protest as it spent its accumulated kinetic energy rotating the engine into self-sustaining life. With twice the horsepower of the PT and much less wind resistance, the BT could easily cruise between 140 and 160 mph.

My first instructor in the BT-13 was 1st Lieutenant Borna, from Long Island, New York. He was an excellent instructor. Similar to most military instructors we had, and were to have from this point on, he was in his late 'twenties or early 'thirties. As in primary, each instructor had about five cadets to teach. Since we had all flown the Stearman primary trainer, none of us was a complete novice. We all knew how it felt.

I cannot remember much about the first few hours of my training, except that I had the utmost respect for Lt. Borna, and I very much liked the Vultee. Because the propeller had so much torque in low pitch, the BT-13 had a decided tendency to turn or bank to the left. This characteristic required the pilot to compensate with appropriate pressure on the right rudder pedal. A favorite maxim was that if you were doing something wrong, "give it more right rudder."

I managed to remember this rule, and I also kept my head moving—"looking around," to make sure other fledgling pilots were not in our air space. All the instructors were very emphatic that we not bury our noses in the cockpit, and they would often forgive other mistakes if we kept alert to what was going on around us.

As with any plane, the novice had first to practice climbs, turns, stalls, and all the rudiments for getting into the air safely and back on the ground in one piece. I felt comfortable with the BT from the beginning, but I did not think about soloing. I just concentrated on learning as much as I could. Lt. Borna was a rigorous taskmaster, but fair and not the least bit vindictive. He had a reputation for putting the BT through quadruple snap rolls.

During my fourth hour of training we were at a grassy practice field a few miles from the main field. The BT we were flying had a distinctive red-and-black checkerboard insignia on the engine cowling. After I had made a few landings, Lt. Borna told me to park the plane near the wind tee and shut down the engine. Then he asked me if I had a handkerchief, which I produced from an interior pocket. He looked at it—it was not too clean—and immediately informed me that I now had five "gigs" (demerits) for a dirty handkerchief. He next told me to blindfold myself with the handkerchief. That accomplished, he gave me a conventional cockpit instrument check. This test required the student to identify all gauges and controls in the cockpit by touch or description. He stood on the wing next to my cockpit while he administered the test.

After I took the blindfold cockpit test and properly passed it, he told me to remove the handkerchief. He then advised me to start the engine and take off, while he stayed on the ground at the wind tee! *He meant for me to solo*! However, before he climbed off the wing, he told me earnestly that if I did anything to screw up he would have my hide, especially the posterior area. My flying reflected his ability as an instructor. If I messed it up, he also was responsible. He need not have feared. Although I had not expected to solo, I knew I was ready and I had no apprehensions.

With my adrenaline near maximum, I went through the pre-flight procedure and started up the engine. I then taxied out to the downwind end of the airstrip and turned the plane into the wind for take-off. Though excitement was surging through me, I remembered to perform the required cockpit check. Finally I was ready. In front of me was a smooth grassy field, probably 3,000 feet long, with a row of trees at the far end. I checked all the instruments and controls again, and ran up the engine to test the magnetos. Then I throttled back and headed the BT-13 into the wind. Exulting in the grandeur of the moment, I poured on full power to that Pratt & Whitney engine. As the BT accelerated and took itself off, the propeller in low pitch announced the event to the sky, the fields, the trees, the birds, and anyone who would listen. I climbed to 1,000 feet, and followed the conventional rectangular landing pattern—downwind leg, base leg, approach to landing, flair out, and land.

I made an excellent landing. As the plane touched down not far from the wind tee where he was watching, Lt. Borna waved his arms signaling me to keep going and do it again. Only too willingly I poured it on, letting the whole world know that Aviation Cadet Timberlake, Richard H., Jr, was soloing the vaunted BT-13. I made two more landings, after which Lt. Borna signaled me to stop and pull up to the tee. He climbed in and we went back to the main field where I made another landing.

By this time the principle of getting the stick back, Back, **Back** into my lap and keeping it there was a part of my personality. Back-into-the-lap worked for everything I flew, even though "everything" was just four different aircraft. The date was 12 October 1943.

I was pleased as punch that I had soloed. I had done so after only a minimal four hours of instruction, and I could now go out and practice on my own.

One of my cadet friends—the one who had initiated the stick-back-in-the-lap method for landings—asked a bunch of us at supper that evening, "Who was flying the BT with the checkerboard nose?" I admitted that I was the one. He then told us that he had been practicing at the same field where I had soloed. He and his instructor had also been parked in their plane near the wind tee. When his instructor witnessed my solo performance, he looked over to Lt. Borna and gave him a big A-ok sign with the thumb and forefinger. So, someone did see me then, if only for a brief moment. Apparently, I had done no damage to Borna's prestige as an instructor.

A/C Timberlake and the BT-13, Greenwood Army Air Base, Mississippi, October 1943

Basic flight training was the highlight of my flying career. The BT-13 was a good solid maneuverable aircraft with good power. It was not a real fighter plane, which I hoped I would fly if I finally earned my wings, but it was getting there. I always regretted that its engine did not have fuel injection like a real fighter plane, so that it would continue to run and produce power even when the plane was upside down. No training planes had fuel injection. Consequently, gas could not flow through the carburetor when the plane was inverted, and the engine would quit until the craft was right side up again. Once right side up, the idling propeller would immediately restart the engine.

Our ground school instructors, and practically everyone else, had told us that the BT-13 was a "vicious spinner." They meant that once it was stalled into a tailspin, stopping the spin and restoring equilibrium was difficult. After I had practiced stalls, getting into spins and getting out again, and had soloed, I decided to check out this widely held belief. So one day when I was on my own, I took my BT up to 6,000 feet—much higher than we usually went for acrobatics. Then, I throttled down the engine and raised the nose 45° to stall out. The plane duly stalled, flipped over on one wing, and started spinning down.

A conventional aircraft in a tailspin is in a state of forced disequilibrium. It is both stalled out, spinning, and descending. Its airspeed indicator shows the stalled out speed, which for the BT was about 60 mph. If the aircraft is truly unstable, the intensity of the spin should become aggravated. With the power off, I let this BT make seventeen complete rotations before I brought it out around 3,000 feet. I popped the stick forward, breaking the stall, and the airspeed increased rapidly. The wing surfaces responded appropriately so that the spin became a straightforward dive, from which that beautiful BT-13 pulled out cleanly. Nothing about it was unusual or unstable. So much for the "vicious spinner" fable.

We practiced many other interesting acrobatics besides tailspins: slow rolls, snap rolls, Immelmans, chandelles, and loops. We also practiced short-field landings over a hurdle. This exercise consisted of bringing the plane in over a flagged rope—a "hurdle"—fixed 16 feet above the ground. The goal was to land as quickly as possible once the plane had cleared the hurdle.

Once in my zest for this exercise, I came in over the hurdle a bit too slow. The plane stalled out before I wanted it to, and too high off the ground. The left wing dropped sickeningly as though it wanted to bury itself in the turf. Desperately, I rammed the throttle to the quadrant-stop, threw the stick to the right, and pushed the right rudder pedal to its limit hoping that the engine, ailerons and rudder would grab hold in time. Gravity had its way. The plane banged down on the left wheel much too hard, fortunately without hitting a wing or doing any real damage. One bounce and the power took hold. The engine roared defiantly, and we were flying again. From then on, I made sure I had enough air speed to get well over the hurdle before I stalled out to land. Although I should have known it by this time, the experience taught me that one cannot force a plane to land any more than one can force it to take off before it is ready.

We also practiced "spot" landings, which consisted of managing the approach to a landing so that the aircraft touched down as close as possible to a whitewashed circle on the ground. We flew at night to practice night landings, and made cross-country flights both day and night.

Hazing was a characteristic of cadet life that the Air Force authorities had phased out by the time I was a cadet. Some of it had been dangerous; some of it was ludicrous; but most of it was the kind of artificial discipline that in later years led to humorous stories and some bizarre tales.

Our flight instructors in basic seemed to regret the abolition of hazing, and let us know that they thought our cadet life had been "too easy." Therefore, when we were out at the flight line in our flying clothes and under their jurisdiction, they gave us a taste of what it had been like, maybe six months or so earlier, when "things were rough."

One day after some minor infraction of flight line procedures had occurred, the senior flight officer called us to "Attention," and started dressing us down for whatever had happened.

"Pre-pre-flight, pre-flight, primary, you've had it too easy," he drawled ominously. "From now on you're going to start doing things Right." He went on in this vein for several minutes, while we all tried to look attentive and properly chastised.

It is possible that I was not properly attentive, perhaps not standing quite straight enough, and Lt. Borna noticed my casual attitude.

"Mr. Timberlake," he rasped. "Yes, sir," I answered.

"How much gas does a BT-13 hold?" he asked. I gave the correct answer, and he pursued the interrogation further.

"What octane rating is the gasoline?" he continued. "Ninety octane, sir," I answered correctly.

"What kind of air do they put in the tires?" he asked sarcastically.

"Free air, sir," I answered smartly, my answer reflecting logos that appeared at most automobile service stations in that era. I think I may have smiled when I said it, and I heard a snicker or two from my fellow cadets who were supposed to be at strict attention.

"Oh," said Lt. Borna. "You think this is funny do you, Mr. Timberlake?" Whereupon he ordered me into an exaggerated position of attention commonly known as a *brace.*

"Get those shoulders back," he barked. "Suck in that gut. Get that head back. Now let me tell you, Misto [common slang for "mister"], knowing the fundamentals of this aircraft isn't funny. You got that?" he roared.

"Yes, sir," I replied from my brace position. I realized that he was probably half in fun and half in earnest, so I accepted his critique both in good faith and in good spirit. After a few more choice remarks, he allowed me to relax. The commandant then turned to other matters. That was my only experience with "bracing." In retrospect, I feel that it was a sort of rite of passage into the "The Club."

The end of our basic flight training came in late November 1943. As a parting exercise, some of us were to participate in a base air show that would feature short-field landings, spot landings, hurdles, and other flight skills. I was one chosen to do spot landings, and I looked forward with much enthusiasm to the pending competition. However, our neat little air show was not to be. Fog settled down on the airfield for three solid days and canceled the exercise completely.

The author in front of barracks, Greenwood Army Air Base, October 1943

Our training at Greenwood finished, we made ready for the transfer to advanced flight training. All of us had been to the same primary and basic training program, but advanced was to be a different story. Some cadets would go to single-engine advanced and fly the North American AT-6 to train as fighter pilots. The remainder would go to twin-engine advanced and fly the Beechcraft AT-10 to train for multi-engine aircraft. Multi-engine meant two-or four-engine planes, such as the C-47, B-17, B-24, B-25, B-26, and the not-yet-known B-29.

The air corps administrative officers in charge of our destinies distributed preference lists that asked what we wanted to fly after we graduated. They guaranteed nothing. (You could say that again!) However, if "feasible," the Air Corps wanted to let us fly the plane we preferred. Besides the "availability" of the aircraft, that is, whether military operations required its presence or not, one other factor was a major determinant: If the cadet was taller than an even six feet, he had to go to twin-engine advanced and ultimately fly "big" planes, i.e., bombers or transports.

I knew about this qualification only too well. I was six feet one-and-a-half inches and, therefore, destined for twin-engine advanced. Nonetheless, I kept requesting single-engine advanced on the preference questionnaires, thinking that "they" might make an exception to the height limitation rule. However, "they" were not making exceptions, and my name duly appeared on the list to go to twin-engine advanced. I decided to appeal this assignment, which meant a personal visit to the Operations Officer to state my case. I mentioned my intention to my friends, and found out that one of them was going to do the same thing. So we decided make the effort together.

We made the necessary arrangements, shined

our shoes, put on our best faces, and made our way to headquarters. The C.O., who heard our case, was surprisingly sympathetic. (He was also the one who had told us at the flight line that we had had it "too easy.") We had known him to be a tough disciplinarian, but fair. He could have told us to follow orders and get out of here, but he did not. He heard our appeals with understanding. Then he pronounced judgement.

"You," he said to my friend, whose name was J.P. Williams and who was just a small fraction of an inch over six feet, "can go to single-engine. We can bend the rule for the quarter-inch that you are over the limit. But you," he said looking at me and my skinny 6-foot, 1½-inch frame, "are too much over the limit. So you must go to twin-engine as assigned."

We acknowledged his decision, saluted, and departed. I was not exactly disappointed because I had sensed that my appeal was not going to work. Not expecting to get the advanced training mode I desired, I had at least satisfied myself by trying. In a letter to my sister Margaret I wrote, "I am rather sick about it [the decision] as I have wanted to go to single-engine [advanced] ever since I've been flying. But I guess I was too tall for it, although there is one student officer a little taller than I who got it. . . . [Aviation cadets who were already commissioned officers could always expect to realize their preferences. Rank definitely had its privileges.] My only hope now to fly something I really like is to get a P-38. [This plane was a twin-engine fighter, built by Lockheed, and known as "The Lightning." Fat chance! Practically no one could get that plane. I hardly saw one throughout the war.] But I'll probably end up in a B-24 or [sic] a B-17 or the like."

It sounds prophetic now—what I wrote in November 1943, a little more than two months before I received my wings, but it was simple logistics. Every bomber or transport plane needed two pilots. In addition, the total number of all kinds of bombers and transports greatly exceeded the number of fighters and other single-engine aircraft. Finally, the attrition rate of bombers was much higher than that of fighters. The arithmetic was all too obvious. "Too tall" did not really mean what it said. It meant: "We do not need many fighter pilots. We need multi-engine pilots, and this phony qualification is our way of fulfilling our needs without putting the matter bluntly." At times afterwards, I had a few opportunities to sit in fighter planes, and in none of them did I feel cramped. In fact, bombers were more difficult to enter and exit than most fighters.

My friend, J.P. Williams, who was from south central Virginia and a most gentlemanly person, was delighted to go on to single-engine advanced. He trained in AT-6s, and in due course received his wings. He then did operational training in P-47s, and went overseas to fly the P-47 fighter-bomber in Italy with the 15th Air Force. Tragically, he was shot down on his tenth mission. So when we do not get what we feel is our due, are we always so badly off? I cannot argue with the results: I lived and J.P. did not. But I certainly wanted to fly that AT-6. As it was, I never flew or even sat in one.

Chapter 5: Advanced Flight Training

My cadet-pilot class left Greenwood, Mississippi, on 5 December 1943, and arrived in Columbus, Mississippi, the same day for advanced twin-engine training. Again, we were quartered in wooden two-story barracks, with bunk beds and limited space for our belongings. Our bunk beds were fixed so as to define little "rooms" that we were supposed to keep clean. Only the common latrine was a conventional room with walls. This arrangement was similar to what we had at Darr Aero Tech, and not nearly as attractive as what we had just left. However, the food at Columbus was a big improvement over that at Greenwood.

The Beechcraft AT-10 was a conventional low-wing monoplane with two wing-mounted 300-horsepower Lycoming radial engines. It had fully retractable landing gear, constant-speed variable pitch propellers, and most of the current navigational and radio equipment. So it was similar in all-important respects to the multi-engine monsters most of us would fly in the future. The instructor-pilot and the student now sat side-by-side in the cockpit, the student on the right where the copilot customarily sits in any two-pilot aircraft.

Since this plane was a two-pilot aircraft, we never soloed, strictly speaking. Once we had shown our instructors that we could take off and land safely, we went out to fly with other cadets, who were our copilots, as we were theirs. Much more of our training now consisted of navigational cross-country flights, night flying, instrument flying, and some formation flying. None of it was acrobatics because the engineers had not designed the AT-10 for such things. In fact, acrobatics were strictly forbidden.

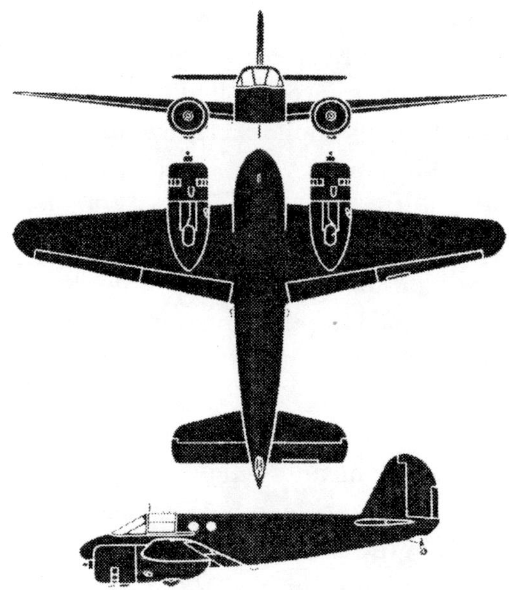

Beechcraft AT-10

One of the more interesting training missions was a 500-mile cross-country flight that we took for navigational training. Our flight plan was very modest by contemporary standards. We were to fly west from Columbus to Vicksburg on the Mississippi River, then turn northwest to Little Rock, Arkansas. After landing, refueling, and lunch, we were to fly straight back to Columbus at "low level," that is, at an altitude of 500 feet. In my immature youth, I did not classify 500 feet as "low level." To me "low level" meant low—maybe 50 feet. What we did not know in our tempestuous youth surely may have hurt us.

I had already decided that for my share of the "low level" leg back to Columbus I was going to get that plane down to what I thought "low level" really meant. So I took off from the field at Little Rock and leveled off at 500 feet. However, as we came over the flatland area of eastern Arkansas, I brought the plane back down to around 200 feet. When I made this adjustment, my copilot, a fellow student who was married, complained vehemently. Nonetheless, I persisted, and I must say it was a memorable experience.

We were at about 200 feet over the lowlands of Arkansas approaching the Mississippi River. It was a mid-January afternoon and we could see workers in the fields, mules, houses, and all the trappings of rural life. Just as we came within sight of the Mississippi River, which meandered its way toward the Gulf of Mexico, we saw a steamboat earnestly churning along much in the same direction as we. As we overtook it, the situation proved too enticing to resist. With my Y-chromosome in high gear, I dropped the AT-10 down to smokestack level for the "buzz-job" on the boat. I could imagine the disconcerted crew excitedly following my script. I was not a complete damn fool: we cleared the top of the boat's stacks by a goodly margin—perhaps 50 feet, and continued across the Mississippi.

Then I noticed something that I never afterwards forgot: Depth perception over water becomes difficult. The water is "too flat"—no trees, no hills, nothing to give a perspective. Something told me not to test this uncertainty any further, and I immediately pulled up to a "reasonable" altitude. I knew only too well what might happen if a propeller dug itself into the water. The river would win that one.

My copilot was much relieved when I regained normal "low level" altitude. Shortly thereafter, it was his turn to fly, and he flew us uneventfully back to our base at Columbus. Fortunately, no one on that steamboat had the idea, or perhaps the means, to report my mischief to the authorities.

The AT-10 was a docile aircraft. It did just what it was supposed to do with very few surprises. It had excellent visibility from the cockpit; it cruised at 170 mph; it would fly level on one engine; and although it did not have superchargers, the instrument cluster included manifold pressure gauges for both engines. This feature was to get us accustomed to dealing with supercharged engines, for all operational planes by this time had them. The only problem of any consequence with the AT-10 was the remote possibility that the landing gear, or just one wheel, would get stuck in the "wheels up" (or "wheels down") position. If this problem occurred, the pilot had to bring the plane in on its belly. I only heard of one such incident while I was at Columbus, and the cadet who carried out the landing did it so skillfully that no harm was done beyond what the plane suffered from skidding to a stop on its belly.

While the AT-10 was fast by the standards of the time, it also had the surprising characteristic of being able to "slow-fly." That is, it would maintain level flight at a speed much less than its normal landing speed, which was perhaps 65 mph. The slow-fly procedure called for full flaps, landing gear down, props in the flattest pitch (like low gear in a car) and engines revved up enough to keep the plane level. The attitude of the plane became decidedly nose-up. The blast of the propellers over the wing surfaces, and especially against the fully extended flaps, kept the plane aloft. Its speed would drop lower and lower until 40 mph showed on the airspeed indicator. Of course, one did not practice this maneuver near the ground, for the flight controls became mushy just as if the plane were stalling. Indeed, it would have stalled instantly with a complete loss of control if the power were cut off. The maneuver was useful knowledge, however, if the plane was in some sort of emergency and had to make a landing in a confined space.

When I first heard of this tactic, I did not believe it. In fact, I think I lost some money on a bet about such a weird capability. Nevertheless, the proof of the pudding is in the experience. I found out afterwards that virtually any plane with flaps and pitch-controlled propellers would slow-fly. The B-17, with a normal landing speed of about 90-95 mph would slow-fly at 80 mph (I found out later) when it was unloaded.

Much of our flying in Advanced consisted of instrument training and navigational cross-country flights. We also practiced some mild maneuvers, such as Lazy Eights, but nothing very interesting. I do not remember even one tailspin.

Near the end of our training, we practiced some formation flying—something many of us would very much need. However, our AT-10 formations were all single-file, stepped-up echelon patterns, a style that none of the operational air forces ever used. In this formation the lead plane is in front and below all the others. Each succeeding plane is above, behind, and to one side of the plane in front. Our instructors had advised us that if we were flying the lead plane, we should never turn toward the formation but always away from it. Failure to follow this principle would give us a "below average" grade for formation flying.

Echelon formation training, and the rule not to turn in toward the formation, proved to be misinformation. In operational flying we never flew echelon patterns, and we turned any which way that was necessary. All of which went to show, as one should expect, that formation flying was best learned by practicing it in the plane one flew operationally.

December 1943 and January 1944 became history. The date for our graduation, 8 February 1944 approached, and with it came all sorts of exciting things. We were to become officers—presumably we were already gentlemen, and we had to buy new uniforms. Our uniform allowance was $ 250, which, in those days of good suits for $ 25, would buy a lot of high quality clothes. However, most of us used all of this allowance and a good bit more. Many of us had never had such "good" clothes as we were now getting. The new uniforms were handsome: forest green blouses, a pair each of "pink" and green wool trousers, and green shirts, all of the finest wool gabardine. We also bought "pink" trench coats of the same material and good khaki shirts and trousers for hot weather. Best of all, above our left breast pocket, shirt or tunic, would be the silver wings of an Air Force PILOT.

We purchased the uniforms and insignia, including the silver wings, at the base Post Exchange (PX). Some of us could not help but notice that a well-endowed female clerk at the PX used a pair of silver wings to fasten her apron in back, but we did not let this slur discomfit us. Why did she do it? Maybe she could not find a safety pin; or maybe she had experienced an unhappy affair with some cadet and was flouting our coveted icon to bedevil us.

By the time I graduated as an Air Force pilot, I had a total of 254 flying hours, 116 hours in advanced, including copilot time, 73 hours in basic, and 65 hours in primary. Approximately 350 cadets graduated in my class of 44-B on 8 February 1944 at Columbus Army Air Base. This number is staggering when one considers that every month another 300 or so would graduate, and that several other advanced flying schools were turning out similar numbers. The total must have been at least 3,000 new pilots a month!

I found out many decades later that this kind of output turned into "overproduction." When no market forces are present to allocate resources, and production is a result of command decisions, specialized resources may be used in most unspecialized ways. As a plethora of pilot trainees congested the training fields a few months later, cadets who had expected to get flight training were suddenly grounded and told that they had no future as pilots in the Air Force. Many of them were reassigned to other services, and others found themselves doing menial ground duty chores simply because the need for their services as pilots had gone to zero. The number of pilots and potential pilots had come to exceed the number of flying berths.

On 7 February 1944, the day before our graduation, we received formal papers that discharged us from the Army. We took off all our cadet insignia and became "civilians" for a night. Lest anyone take advantage of this technicality by packing up and going home, we were informed that induction into the infantry would follow such hanky-panky the day after tomorrow. Anyway, it did mean we could go out and have a beer with our instructors if they so chose.

For reasons that no one ever explained to us, perhaps 10 per cent of the graduates became Flight Officers instead of Second Lieutenants. The Flight Officer rank was similar to a Warrant Officer in the regular army. It was a rank something like an exalted sergeant—a noncommissioned officer who had commissioned officer status and privileges, but somehow was not an officer. Instead of the gold bar of a second lieutenant, the Flight Officer wore a blue bar with rounded corners and a gold stripe through the center. No one in authority ever revealed to us the reasons or conditions for the Flight Officer rank. The day before we graduated, some cadets had a special notice on their bunks informing them that they would be Flight Officers. All it seemed to mean in practice was that such an officer's first promotion would be to Second Lieutenant rather than to First Lieutenant.

Our graduation ceremony did not amount to much; it was very perfunctory. Some few of my colleagues had wives or family members present who could pin on their wings and Second Lieutenant bars, but most of us did it for each other. Not many civilians had the means then to make a trip for such an "unnecessary" reason. Federal government rationing of gasoline and all forms of travel were so severe that traveling more than a few miles was very difficult, and officially frowned upon by ration boards. Most of our families were 500 to 1,000 miles to the north, so we celebrated with our comrades.

In retrospect, I believe that this way was the best and the most natural because we all knew what our friends had been through. Parents and family might have been "proud" of us, but they could never be part of our new "family." Our common experience for the last year had been with our fellow cadets. Our real families could not share that experience no matter how close we were to them. No doubt, this condition has existed from the beginning of time, and so it will ever be.

After the ceremony at which we formally became officers, gentlemen, and pilots, we signed each other's sacred photo books: "See you in the wild blue yonder over Berlin (or Tokyo)," we wrote. Or we penned some witticism that recalled a familiar incident: "Don't ground loop that B-17." Or, "Keep your wings level and true." Then we packed up our new uniforms in our newly acquired A-2 garment bags and B-3 duffel bags, and departed the Columbus Army Air Base by whatever means we could muster. All of us had orders to report to such-and-such a base or field for assignment to fly some kind of operational plane after a "delay en route of 10 days." My orders read that I was to report to the "3rd AF [Air Force] Replacement Depot, Plant Park, Tampa, Florida," and an accompanying document stated:

"Orders necessitated asgmt [assignment] to B-25s." (Fifty-six years later, I still have those yellowed mimeographed papers.) Twenty-six of us who had just graduated had identical orders sending us to Tampa for "assignment in B-25s." The B-25 seemed to me a reasonable compromise between what I wanted to fly (fighters) and the worst that I might get (four-engine heavy bombers). Yes, a reasonable compromise. But don't forget, Lt. Timberlake: This is the army!

Chapter 6: Operational Training in the B-17

After the graduation ceremony, all of us newly minted pilots suddenly realized that we had 10 days leave but few good travel options to get from Columbus, Mississippi, to the many far away places we wanted to reach. A race for travel accommodations erupted. Fortunately, I was quick enough to get a commercial plane ticket from Columbus to Birmingham, and then to Cincinnati. From there I traveled by bus through Ohio, visiting family and friends for several days. I then took a train through Washington, D.C. to Tampa, Florida, and arrived on the day prescribed by my orders, 21 February 1944.

My new base, and that of dozens of other pilots, bombardiers, and aircrew personnel, was a "tent city" in Plant Park, a minor league baseball field. The Cincinnati Reds baseball team had used this field for their spring training practice prior to the opening of the major league baseball season.

The tents were truly tents in that they had canvass roofs. However, they also had slatted wooden sides and wooden floors, so were reasonably comfortable until the weather got summery. Since it was late February, the weather was ideal. We thus enjoyed an environment for which well-to-do people spent much money in the effort to escape the rigor of northern winters.

The morning after I arrived, an operations officer from Third Air Force Headquarters called an assembly of all the just arrived pilots. A rumor that we were not going to fly the plane we had expected to fly—the North American B-25—was by this time all but an accepted fact, and the officer immediately confirmed it.

"How many of you," he asked, "came down here with the understanding that you would fly B-25s?"

All of us who had graduated from Columbus Army Air Base raised our hands.

"Well," he said, "your assignment has been changed. Your new job is to train as copilots on B-17s." And that was that. Yes, this is the Army, Lt. Timberlake!

This announcement was most unwelcome, especially to me, since I had my eyes open the whole time and would have preferred almost any other flying assignment. I sensed the futility of trying to get things changed, but I was sorry afterward that I did not make the attempt then and there.

When one has been regimented long enough, he begins to believe that his individual preferences will never be honored. Why should the authorities have made an exception for me when they could not do the same for everyone else? One assumes this restriction intuitively when he is part of the affected group, so he feels embarrassed not to go along with what has been prescribed. I had already tried to go to single-engine advanced and had been denied. Later I would try again and, of course, again would be turned down. However, if I had been insistent enough when I first arrived at Plant Park, I might have had a chance.

For the next six weeks we led an idyllic existence at Plant Park. We played some war games and had other light duties just to keep us busy. We also had lots of time off to play softball and volleyball, and to enjoy the surroundings—the beaches, the nightlife of Tampa, and the weather. Most of us were northerners who had not traveled very far beyond our own states' boundaries. So a vacation in Florida was not hard to take.

Inevitably, the idyll had to end. The end came on 30 March, when orders were posted that organized us into crews and assigned us to Drew Field, an operational training base for B-17s a few miles outside Tampa. We were to report for duty on 2 April.

Before we left for Drew, however, we assembled in crew-clusters of nine men: pilot, copilot, bombardier, top turret gunner-engineer, radio operator, two waist gunners, one of whom was the armorer, ball turret gunner, and tail gunner. The navigators would add another member to each crew, but they did not arrive until a few days later.

All of us were a little embarrassed when we first met in the hot March sun that day in Plant Park. Forty-three crews were on the orders to go to Drew, so it took an effort to get everyone together in the right place. Finally we congregated into crews, and everyone had the chance to size up the others. I cannot remember having either positive or negative first impressions about my fellow crewmembers. To assume anything would have been foolish. We had to believe that everyone else was properly trained and capable, so why speculate? The proof of the pudding would come when we started flying.

GI trucks promptly transported us to Drew Field. The officers—pilots, copilots, bombardiers and (later) navigators—were housed in small cement block barracks. Each crew was in a separate 'apartment' containing three rooms. Latrines, with showers, washing facilities and toilets were in separate buildings behind the living quarters.

Everything about Drew Field seemed temporary, and it was. Nonetheless, the training there was serious, and a hot and tedious business. Each crew had to practice as a unit, which meant that everyone had to coordinate his specialty with what his fellow crewmembers were doing. Necessarily, some of us had much more to learn than the others.

First, an experienced senior pilot had to check out our first pilot to be sure that he could handle the plane and manage the crew. The pilot then coordinated the rest of the crew's duties. As copilot, I had to learn to fly the plane properly, following the pilot's instructions and suggestions. Our bombardier was to practice his bombing skills, using 100-pound, sand-filled practice bombs, and the navigator had to be constantly aware of our position and where we were going. Gunners, some of whom had other functions besides manning a pair of .50-caliber machine guns, were to practice their gunnery and their other assigned specialties. The top turret gunner, for example, was also the engineer and had to know the details of the plane's technical structure. Our operational training was to take two months, April and May 1944.

So we began a seemingly endless round of flying activities—takeoffs, landings, practice bomb runs, navigational flights, and gunnery practice over the Gulf of Mexico. Machine gun practice, both air-to-air against targets towed by fighter planes, and air-to-ground at water targets in the Gulf of Mexico, was especially interesting. I even had my turn firing the top turret guns at a target sleeve towed by a fighter plane. I also fired one of the waist guns at a water target as we circled above it, and could see the bullets splashing in the water. Suddenly, the gun I was firing "ran away" on me. I had probably squeezed the trigger longer than was advisable, so it would not stop firing until the ammunition belt ran out of .50-caliber slugs. (The prescribed time for a burst was two seconds so that the gun could cool before the next burst.) It was not a dangerous situation because the bullets went harmlessly into the water. Thereafter, I concentrated on flying.

We were labeled the "Locker crew" because our pilot was Lawrence G. Locker, and common practice was to name a crew after the last name of the pilot. The other members of the crew, besides me, were: Jack Moss, bombardier; Gene Finucane, navigator; Delbert Breedlove, engineer and top turret gunner; John Wingfield, armorer and waist gunner; Bob Walsh, radio operator; John Coco, ball turret gunner; Jack Sweet, waist gunner, and Fred Stoker, tail gunner.

Locker had trained in B-17s at Lockbourne Air Base near Columbus, Ohio, for two months before his assignment to Plant Park. He had learned his lessons well, and was very conscientious. He was, in fact, a perfect example of what a bomber pilot should be. I immediately respected what he was and what he did, even while I cursed my luck at finding myself in a berth that I detested and had tried to avoid. I had no illusions about the vulnerability of the B-17 and where we were headed. The only thing worse would have been a B-24, or being in the infantry. I always sympathized with those boys.

The pilot was the crew leader and in command. He knew far more about the plane and its operating principles than anyone else. The copilot was only in charge if the pilot was somehow incapacitated. At some future time, he might aspire to the role of first pilot if he had some ambition for the job. I had no interest in such a position. Compared to the role I fancied for myself as a fighter pilot, my copilot job was a bitter pill to swallow.

With all this disappointment, I was at least realistic. I could not do anything about my unhappy lot, but as a matter of self-preservation I had to learn as much as I could about the plane and its operating procedures. Somewhere, sometime in the future, several lives, including my own, might depend on how well I learned my lessons now.

Our first training mission on 7 April 1944 was also my first flight in a B-17. The senior pilot to check out Locker was in the copilot seat, while I stood behind the two pilots as an observer. After two flights with the check pilot, Locker satisfied the requirements for being the aircraft commander. From this time on we flew as a crew, I in the copilot seat, without oversight by anyone.

Most of my training in the B-17 was on my own. The Air Corps had no program for copilots who, I found out much to my amazement, were regarded as second class pilots. They existed only as backups to spell the first pilots, and to carry out other menial duties, such as helping the pilot start the engines. Locker, I am pleased to say, never had this attitude. However, it surfaced repeatedly during my B-17 flying career, and it always surprised and offended me. I expected to be judged on the merits of my flying, not on some elitist notion that saw copilots as inferior just because they had the bad luck to fall into the copilot seat. It was not as if the Air Corps had conducted tests to decide who should fly as pilot and who as copilot. It was all sheer logistics at this stage of the war: B-17 pilots were those who had stated in twin-engine advanced that they wanted to fly B-17s. Copilots were primarily those who had stated a preference for other flying berths that were not available. Perhaps other factors entered the picture, too, but if so no one ever explained them. Certainly, no cadet ever stated on a preference form that he wanted to be a copilot on a B-17! Maybe while in training those who ultimately became copilots did not display proper "maturity" or some similar characteristic. My continued insistence that I wanted to fly fighters no doubt contributed to my ultimate role as a bomber copilot. However, I am sure that a stated preference for bombers and simple logistics were the primary determinants.

The generally low esteem for copilots was ironic because the B-17 was so easy to fly. I knew from the first time Locker gave me the controls that flying it would be child's play. It had no "bugs." It was slow as hob, but it was reliable, tough, and predictable. After I had the controls a few times, I concluded that I could have flown it right after I had finished primary training. I am glad I did not do so, but it was that easy to fly. On the other hand, the budding copilot had much important technical information to learn about the plane. Flying it was one thing; knowing it was something else.

After we flew a few times together, Locker let me take off and land the plane on my own. Takeoffs were a test of patience, not so much in our operational training when the planes were never loaded to capacity, but later in England, where we would sweat them out on cold, dark windless mornings. Even in training at Drew Field, the B-17 needed plenty of runway.

The procedure for aircraft operation required a number of pre-flight checks of equipment and aircraft components even before we started the engines. Once these housekeeping chores were finished, we would start the engines in sequence, beginning with the outboard engine on our left, and continuing in order to the outboard engine on our right. Starting procedure was similar to what it had been in our training planes, except that we now had four engines to deal with instead of one or two.

The controls for starting the engines were on the floor at the copilot's left. When the pilot ordered, "Start One," I would turn a lever with four numbered engine settings to "One" and move a toggle switch to "Energize." Again, as in the training planes, a flywheel would build up speed to a high whine, whereupon the pilot would order, "Contact." On his order I would turn the switch handle to "Mesh," while he switched on the magnetos to provide ignition, and the flywheel would revolve the engine into life. Each engine was started the same way. The pilot then adjusted the throttles so that the engines warmed up at 1,000 revolutions per minute (rpm). We then went through another check of the engines and the plane, running up each engine to check magnetos, turbo-superchargers, propeller pitch, and several other things. If everything mechanical was O.K., we taxied out to the assigned runway for take-off with other planes lined up preparing to do the same thing.

The pilot had all four throttle levers in his right hand and his left hand on the "stick," or yoke—a half-wheel mounted on a stout steel cylindrical arm about three inches in diameter. For the copilot the hand functions were reversed. My left hand held the throttle handles, which were between the pilot and me, and my right hand held the control wheel. When it was our turn to go, the pilot slowly advanced ("walked") the four throttle handles forward until all the engines were at maximum power. Then, he released the brakes and the B-17 started moving.

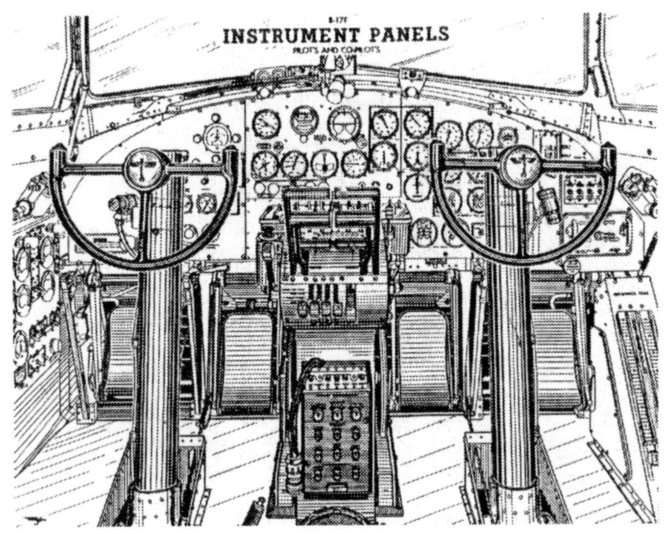

Schematic cockpit view of B-17 showing dash panel and flight controls

"Maximum power" for our engines was 46 inches of manifold pressure, which meant a 53 per cent "boost" over normal sea level pressure of 30 inches. The engines received this boost from exhaust-driven turbo superchargers. Propellers were set at their lowest pitch so that they turned at 2500 rpm for maximum acceleration. The flight engineer, standing behind and between the pilots, called out the plane's speed as it gathered momentum and lift. All the pilot had to do was keep the nose aligned with the runway by using the rudder pedals, . . . and wait . . . and wait . . . and wait. Wind noise and metal resonance built up with the plane's momentum. At an indicated speed of 110-115 mph, a fully loaded B-17 had the necessary lift to get off the ground.

At take-off the tail of the B-17 did not noticeably come up first in the fashion of training planes and most other aircraft of the period. The B-17 lifted off in almost a three-point attitude. However, one had to be patient. Force it off the ground with the elevators before it had enough airspeed to remain airborne and 33 tons of plane and nine men could become statistics. If the plane was running out of runway, the pilot could turn up the superchargers two more notches to "war emergency power." This increase gave the engines an extra turbo-boost, but at the cost of stressing them beyond their normal limits. Wing flaps could also be lowered 20 degrees to give extra lift. Take-off weight fully loaded "for business" was 65,500 pounds—almost 33 tons. The four 1200-horsepower Wright Cyclone engines, each with a Hamilton, three bladed, variable pitch propeller, provided the thrust.

If take-off was simple but sometimes agonizingly slow, landing was child's play. The B-17's big broad wings allowed slow and gentle landings. The approach-to-landing airspeed was 125 mph. As the plane came in toward the runway with full flaps down, it always seemed to me like a giant umbrella. Touchdown speed was only 90 mph. Just as the wheels at take-off had left the ground together, so they usually touched the runway simultaneously on landing. In fact, the tail wheel could easily touch before the main landing wheels, but the proper way was three-point. Once the B-17 touched down, the pilot could push the "stick" full forward and apply as much pressure to the brakes through the medium of the rudder pedals as he wished. This maneuver brought the plane to a rapid stop. Pushing the "stick" forward, as if to dive the plane, took weight off the tail and put it on the wheels, which had the brakes, so that they would grab the landing surface. This tactic never caused a nose-over because the tail was so heavy. Most often, however, we just let the plane slow down of its own accord.

The procedure mentioned above was for short field landings. It was so effective, however, that I often thought that an empty B-17 could have landed on an aircraft carrier. Say that a carrier is making 20 knots and headed into a 15-knot wind. A B-17 landing on it would have had a relative speed to the carrier of about 50 mph: 90 mph-23 mph carrier speed-17 mph of head wind. An empty B-17, once on a carrier deck, could easily slow to zero from 50 mph in less than 500 feet. Carrier landing decks typically measure about 850 feet. This length would have been plenty to accommodate a B-17, even though the B-17 did not have a tail hook. Just a thought for the ages.

The heat and humidity at Drew Field became most unpleasant in May and June. We often went out to the flight line in the early afternoon for missions to practice formation flying at "altitude," which meant somewhere between 10,000 and 16,000 feet. The planes, bathed in the Florida sun all morning, would have interiors like ovens. Toting heavy flying suits into such ghastly heat seemed unbearable, but the temperature at 16,000 feet was going to be just under freezing. So if we relied on nothing more than our leather A-2 jackets, we would be teeth-chattering wrecks by the time we landed some four hours later. Unbearable or not, we carried our fleece-lined flying suits with us and gladly put them on at altitude.

I learned to fly the B-17 as well as many of the first pilots while we were at Drew, and I think the other copilots did, too. However, I did not know the B-17 as well as most of the pilots, and I had no aspirations to become a first pilot. Locker strongly influenced my learning program. As he said, it was in his self-interest to have a copilot who could handle the ship.

We were still at Drew Field on D-day, 6 June 1944. To us, the invasion was a spectator event just as it was to civilians. We hoped that it presaged the beginning of the end, but we had no real understanding of the destruction and horror that accompanied it. Some of us may even have felt a little disappointed that the war might be all over before we had a chance to get our licks in. I hope I was not one such, for I would have lived to rue such a thought.

2nd Lieutenant Richard Timberlake, B-17 copilot, Drew Field, May 1944

Chapter 7: Overseas Deployment and the Approach to Combat

Our operational training ended on 18 June 1944, when we received orders to report to Hunter Field, Savannah, Georgia, by 23 June. Forty-four crews, more than 400 men, were subject to this order. We arrived at Hunter on schedule the day before my 22nd birthday.

Hunter Field was a "staging" area—a transitional base with a constant flow of men in and men out, and the next-to-the-last stop on the way overseas. Here we received our final medical inoculations, and had photographs taken that would identify us as "European civilians" if we were shot down and became pedestrians in occupied territory. We also made final preparations for "the worst"—you know, insurance and that sort of thing, just in case our trip over turned out to be one-way. We also received a final five-day leave that began 1 July and ended 6 July. Even as this last dispensation was granted, we had orders calling for our transport to Camp Kilmer, New Jersey, to arrive by 10 July, " . . . for temp[orary] duty pending further dispatch to overseas destination thru New York or Boston P[ort]/[of] E[mbarkation]. . . ." The orders reflected the drama of what was happening to us: "This is a PERMANENT change of station to an overseas destination. . . ." No dependents were to accompany us or be anywhere near us. We were not to discuss when or where we were going. We would get an APO (Army Post Office) number for our new address, which would be somewhere overseas—for us, England. Forty-eight crews were included in this order.

I.D. issued at Camp Kilmer

Camp Kilmer at New Brunswick, New Jersey, was essentially a turnstile through which flowed soldiers, airmen, nurses, WACs, service groups and others, to be put on ships and transported to England. Our ship was the British liner, *Aquitania*, which we boarded on 14 July 1944, for the trip across the Atlantic.

Our voyage was a most interesting experience for all of us, especially to someone such as I, who had never seen an ocean, a huge ship, the British Navy in action, or just about anything else in the big wide world. I daresay most of my fellow airmen were in much the same (of course) boat.

The *Aquitania* was similar to the notorious *Titanic* in that it had four stacks and was about the same size. However, it was not technically a "sister ship" to the *Titanic*. According to Locker's record of the trip, the *Aquitania* was 902 feet long and weighed more than 45,000 tons. It traveled at 24 knots, and without escort ships.

Life on board for the five-day crossing of the Atlantic was almost idyllic. Officers were berthed eight to a cabin, while enlisted men, as Locker put it, were "stacked like cords of wood" in the lower deck. We had two meals a day—breakfast before eight o'clock and dinner at six. If one missed breakfast by sleeping a little too late, he had a long wait until dinner. Peanuts and candy bars at the ship's P.X. were the only supplements available. All our meals were in the ship's big dining room with traditional linen, crystal, and impeccable British waiters. It was our first experience of fish-for-breakfast (cod), and it was the best food I had experienced thus far in military service. I am not hard to please, but some of the food I had while in training was just awful—for instance, hamburger meatballs that you could bounce off the wall.

Every day around noon we had a "general quarters" of sorts that called for all the troops to assemble on the decks for an emergency drill. We could then see what a mass of humanity we were. After the British commanders gave us instructions for emergency actions in case of submarine attack, an American officer read the world news of the day over the ship's public address system. Otherwise we would not have had any inkling of what was happening, since we had no radios, newspapers, or telephones.

Whoever read the news was doing such a botched-up job of it that one of my copilot friends, Bob Voertman, who had worked as an announcer for a college radio station, went to the officer in charge of this detail and had himself installed as newscaster. From then on the reports were intelligible, as Bob was a huge improvement over the previous announcer.

We saw lots of ocean. The big ship was obviously fast and made a zigzag pattern over the water. The British knew all about enemy submarines. We could see the observers scanning the sea constantly for signs of a periscope. When we were about three days out of New York, we saw an observation plane at a distance (I think a B-24), so we knew we were well monitored. Overall, it turned out to be a pleasant cruise on a luxury ocean liner during the best tourist time of the year. We had entertainment as well. Some USO (United Service Organization) groups—dance bands and such—were on their way to Europe to do their thing for the troops. One band was Spike Jones's "City Slickers." Card games were also popular, and went on until early in the morning.

We had been traveling east of course, but also north. I do not know how close we came to Greenland and Iceland. However, the first land we saw was Ireland as we made our way along its northern coast and entered the North Channel. Our destination was Greenock, Scotland, which is on the Firth of Clyde. As we steamed through the North Channel on a sunny, windy afternoon toward Greenock, the ship's speakers suddenly burst into "God Save the King." It was an inspiring moment.

The ship anchored in the harbor at Greenock and we disembarked. We then boarded a train and were transported to the Air Corps Replacement Depot at Stone on Trent in west central England. We spent about a week at the Stone "repple-depple," as it was dubbed, and the experience was uninspiring. The weather even in mid-July was raw and uncomfortable, and the food was terrible. We had little to do beyond taking care of our personal equipment and writing letters.

Americans labeled toilet and bath houses "latrines," while the English called them "ablus," short for ablutions, or cleansings. One afternoon I was taking a shower in the ablu at Stone, and happened to look casually out of the head-high window that provided daylight for the shower. Much to my surprise, I found myself face-to-face with a B-24 Liberator coming head-on and seemingly at my level. The plane must have been no more than 25 or 30 feet above the ground as it roared past. I heard later that a combat crew had just finished its missions and was celebrating its survival. Apparently, one had to do something silly after he had escaped with his skin intact—even risking his skin again in a senseless maneuver. I am not passing judgment; I would probably have done something similar.

About 27 July 1944, British Railways transported us, along with several dozen other crews, across central England into East Anglia, and distributed us piecemeal at four or five Eighth Air Force bomber bases. Our crew and seven others were assigned to the 388th Bomb Group, which was located next to the village of Knettishall in the heart of East Anglia.

For obvious reasons dozens of bomber bases dotted East Anglia. The area was flat and sandy, and therefore suitable for airfields and flying. It was also proximate to the continent of Europe, with only the North Sea between "them" and us.

Ours was a typical bomb group. It included four squadrons of air combat crews, the 560th, 561st, 562nd, and 563rd. Incoming crews were assigned to a squadron to replace crews that had either been shot down or finished their tours and gone home.

Yes, finishing a tour was possible. Early in the air war, say, between the late summer of 1943 and through the spring of 1944, a tour had been 25 missions. The first crew to achieve this goal was that of the oft-celebrated Memphis Belle. By the time we arrived on the scene, the development and tactical use of the P-47 and P-51 long-range fighter escort for the bomber formations had largely defeated the Luftwaffe. As a result, ever more bomber crews were finishing their 25 missions and going home. Some airmen even volunteered to come back and fly a second tour, which was typically 20 additional missions.

In true catch-22 fashion the Eighth Bomber Command raised the mission tour to thirty. Then, came

D-day, 6 June 1944. The ground forces that had been building up combat capital in England but had not been actively engaged, suddenly became the feature attraction—and properly so. Before D-day the Eighth and Ninth Air Forces had been the only acts in town, and the shows had been dramatic. After D-day, the ground forces came center stage. Everyone knew that the war could not be ended—I hesitate to say "won"—until the allied armies had advanced into Germany and routed the German armies. With the Luftwaffe compromised because of the oil shortage in Germany and the overwhelming numbers of American aircraft roaming German skies, German fighter attacks became largely token raids. The air war seemed largely over, so the mission tour was again raised in July 1944, this time to 35 missions.

The invasion also added greatly to the necessity for military awards and decorations to reward the valor and bravery of the ground forces, as would be expected. It thus diluted the "monopoly" that the Air Forces had enjoyed on both the possible circumstances that would lead to acts of bravery, and to the awards and decorations for the same. I do not believe that the various combat forces had quotas for medals signifying extraordinary individual achievement. Nonetheless, before D-day, the events and circumstances of the air war were unique in the European Theater. No other military activities, except occasional commando raids into France, were comparable. After D-day, the ground war eclipsed the air war. Coincidentally, the air war seemed to have been "won." So both by comparison and through circumstance, possible achievements that would have justified Air Force decorations in the past greatly diminished.

One example that supports this argument was the change in the award of the Distinguished Flying Cross (DFC) to bomber crews. Before D-day, every crew member who finished a tour of combat missions received a DFC simply for completing his tour no matter what else he did or did not do to earn it, or what other awards he received. Shortly after D-day, that policy changed. Thereafter, the award of the DFC for finishing a tour of missions was no longer automatic. In fact, it became a very rare event. It was still awarded for extraordinary acts of valor, but here, too, other variables were important. More on this subject later.

Our first few days at the base of the 388th Bomb Group were spent going to ground school, getting oriented, and taking care of other routine matters. On 29 July, before we had even begun to fly practice missions, our crew was walking near the flight line after carrying out some sort of administrative requirement. As we walked along we noticed a solitary B-17 approaching the field, and obviously in some kind of trouble. While we watched it enter the traffic pattern and prepare to land, we saw a large object fall from it. I thought a propeller had come loose, and I said as much. Other crewmembers thought it was one of the machine guns—perhaps doubting that something as important as a prop would just come loose and fall off. The plane's markings showed that it was not from our base.

In fact, a propeller had come off. The plane was returning from a mission on which it had suffered flak damage, and it was trying to make an emergency landing. Since one prop had come off, it had no more than three engines functioning and possibly fewer. As the crippled plane banked in over us and straightened out to land, it disappeared from our view behind a small rise in the ground. We thought it was safely down. However, a few seconds later we saw a huge billow of black smoke rushing into the sky. The plane had landed short of the runway, hit a gas truck and mechanics' tent with ground crew personnel inside, and a parked plane. Strangely enough, we did not hear an explosion.

All of us were on foot. We started to run over the hill for a better view and to see if we could help, but something held us back. Maybe we did not want to see any more, because what had happened was bound to be tragic. We also knew that emergency operations were already in full gear and that we could not possibly help. As it turned out, three men died in the accident, and two planes and a gas truck were destroyed.

Remains of two B-17s and fuel truck after collision, 30 July 1944

I never found out why the pilot could not get the plane down in a better place and in a better mode. Even with only two engines functioning an empty B-17 could maintain altitude and land properly. I never learned any more of the details in this case. So how this incident became a disaster will always be a puzzle.

We started flying practice missions on the last day of July 1944, and the first time we had flown since 15 June at Drew Field in Florida. For the next ten days we flew many more practice missions, and had much other training on enemy aircraft identification, flak defenses, emergency procedures, and all the rest. Often we could hear the groups of bombers forming over our base, their cadenced rumble reaching into every corner of our existence. Practice did not mean perfect, but finally it did mean that our turn had come. Accordingly, in the first week of August 388th Bomb Group headquarters placed us on the roster of crews qualified to fly combat missions.

Chapter 8: My Five Missions with the Locker Crew

We flew our first mission on 11 August 1944. The target was the railroad marshalling yard at Mulhouse, which geographically is in Germany but almost at the common point where France, Germany and Switzerland meet. The strategy of the mission was to disrupt rail communications in anticipation of the Allied landings in southern France that were scheduled to take place a few weeks later. Mulhouse was only a few miles from the Belfort "Gap," where the Allied armies eventually went into southwest Germany. Of course, we common "soldiers" did not know what was afoot.

Our plane was part of a twelve-plane squadron made up of four elements in Vees of three planes.

Each bomb group flew 12-ship squadrons in three formations—lead, high and low, and each squadron had a lead element, and three other three-plane elements, with the squadron leader at the point of the front Vee. The lead plane, and also the deputy lead flying off the right wing of the lead plane, was specially equipped with a radar "dome" in the place normally occupied by the lower ball turret. This trade-off meant that the two lead planes did not have lower ball turret guns to defend themselves from below in case of enemy fighter attack.

All the Vee-element leaders flew off some dimension of the lead plane, and every other plane in each Vee flew off its own element lead. At the target all bombardiers in the formation toggled out their bombs when the lead plane's bombardier, who used his Norden bomb sight, aimed and dropped the lead plane's bombs. The lead plane's bomb release included a smoke flare to signal the other bombardiers to toggle. Thus, Eighth Air Force "precision bombing" was all in the nose of the lead plane. No bombardiers in the rest of the 12-plane squadron individually aimed and dropped bombs. If the weather was cloudy so that the target was obscured, the lead plane dropped its bombs with the aid of its radar. This device was formally labeled a "Pathfinder," but popularly known as a "Mickey."

Eighth Air Force bomber formations were a succession of 36-plane groups, normally, three squadrons per group and 12 planes per squadron. Ordinarily, 25 to 40 groups would take part in a mission—that is, 900 to 1,400 bombers. Each B-17 started with 2,700 gallons of 100-octane gasoline, and three tons of bombs. So a normal mission used up around 3,000,000 gallons of gas. One thousand B-17s cost about $ 300,000,000, or (at least) three billion year-2000 dollars. Such capital costs, which do not include the value of the human capital in the planes, are formidable. The lesson should be clear: You better have plenty of expendable capital around if you want to fight a war, and also a lot of unattached healthy young men.

The mission to Mulhouse was a model of "milk runs." We organized our formations over England and climbed on course as we flew south through France. The day was warm and sunny. Snow-covered peaks of the French and Swiss Alps were clearly visible, including Mont Blanc. No enemy fighters appeared. We bombed from 19,000 feet, the lowest bombing altitude of any mission I would fly. I did not see one flak burst on the bomb run. We returned to England along the same route we had followed in.

Needless to say, this mission was not typical. We received credit for one mission toward completing our tour; but we sensed, and veteran airmen confirmed, that this experience was not what we would experience on future missions.

Our second mission was to Ludwigshaven on the Rhine River to bomb a synthetic oil refinery. The date was 14 August 1944, just 30 years to the day after World War I had begun. We formed over England and flew south through eastern France with the Rhine River on our left. Our group was in the middle of a bomber chain of perhaps 1,200 planes. Each group was two minutes behind the group in front, so we could only see about three groups in front of us. The rest were lost in the distance.

On this day we were at 24,000 feet, and were to bomb going northeast. Consequently, as we arrived near the target flying south, the groups that had bombed ahead of us were headed northeast away from the area while we were still flying toward the target. As we looked at the returning formations heading in the opposite direction, we saw a huge black cloud—perhaps thousands of spent anti-aircraft (flak) bursts. Since we were going past and away from the flak, we had no immediate cause for alarm.

I wonder now why and how we thought we could avoid that flak. We were not up there just for the ride. Our lack of concern was shaken slightly as we saw the several formations immediately in front of us turn ninety degrees toward the east. Our naivete ended forever shortly thereafter. For by this time the forward formations had reached what was called the Initial Point (IP) of the bomb run. Once again the formations turned left ninety degrees, and now their course—and ours—was straight toward the flak. We were inescapably in line behind them. The spent flak bursts loomed in front of us. How, we wondered, could any plane get through that? We soon found out, although in another sense we never found out.

Flak, which is simply called shrapnel when it is directed at ground targets, began to pop up in front of us. Each burst featured a large plume of black smoke out the top and a smaller one out the bottom. The spray of metal to the sides was minimal, and by far the most damage came from the top of the burst. Often a battery of flak guns fired a salvo of about five or six shells that would pop up one above the other. I sometimes thought of this phenomenon as "stepladder" flak. The August air was clear so the flak gunners had a full view of us. As the flak came close, we could hear it explode above the roar of the engines, and often we flew through the smoke of spent bursts.

Strangely enough, the first experience of this kind, due to its novelty, is often not nearly as terrifying as subsequent episodes. An airman observing the spectacle is still sitting in the front row of a theater watching a war movie. He is not yet a part of the action.

As we breached the flak on a straight and level course toward the target, a synthetic oil plant ten miles ahead and five miles below, the pilot suddenly exclaimed to me over the intercom: "Help me hold this thing." The control wheel was pulling forward because flak had severed the elevator trim tab control cable in the waist of the plane. Elevators are airfoils and therefore provide lift as fast-moving air flows over their surfaces. This lift on the elevator forces the tail up and the nose down. An elevator trim tab, however, is set to put constant downward pressure on the elevator, which translates into back pressure on the pilot's control wheel in the cockpit, to prevent the plane from diving. The cable to the tab control being cut, the lift on the elevator tended to force the tail up and the nose of the plane down. I added my strength to Locker's to put back pressure on the wheel that now had more than sixty pounds of force pulling against us. Together, we could muscle the elevator control so that the aircraft maintained level flight.

Suddenly the plane heaved up, and we heard the bombardier, Jack Moss, call out, "Bombs away!" The whole formation, like a school of fish, immediately started a diving turn to the left, dropping a thousand feet very rapidly, and taking us out of the flak. Once we were again in straight and level flight, I reached down to the automatic pilot control switches between the pilots' seats and flipped on the unit's elevator control switch. This device put all the elevator pressure on the elevator servo control, and thereby relieved us of our burden. I could now turn a small knurled knob on the automatic pilot control panel to make the plane climb or descend.

From this point on, I managed the elevators while the pilot continued to fly the plane with rudder, ailerons, and throttles in the usual manner. We stayed in the formation, but at a prudent distance from other planes because our control could not be precise enough for close formation flying. When we arrived at our base, we shut off the auto pilot and landed the plane together. I acted as the elevator trim tab applying back pressure on the stick so that Locker had little difficulty making a normal landing. I think we could have landed the plane with the auto pilot controlling the elevators, but that is now an untestable hypothesis. It is more a commentary on the aerodynamic simplicity of the B-17.

On 16 August, two days later, we were briefed for a mission to bomb another synthetic oil refinery near Zeitz, a town close to Leipzig. The weather was clear and sunny. We assembled in the usual manner over England, and climbed en route toward Germany. Our altitude for the bomb run was to be 21,500, and we were to approach the target from the east.

The most unfortunate part of this mission occurred just before the bomb run. We were flying straight and level in clear weather approaching the target area, and no flak had yet appeared. Our plane was flying the left wing of the low element lead. That is, our three-plane Vee was directly beneath—say, 30 or 40 feet, and behind—perhaps 20 or 30 feet, the lead Vee of our 12-ship squadron. Suddenly without warning and for no apparent reason, the left-wing plane of the lead-element Vee directly above us began drifting down into our air space. It approached our plane from above and our left. At first, this maneuver was nothing to be concerned about. It was not violent, and seemed like an ordinary formation adjustment. Usually, a prompt return to the conventional alignment followed such a tactic.

But not this time. Locker was flying and therefore concentrating on our element lead plane to our right, piloted by Lieutenant Sarten. The vagrant plane was approaching from our left and was out of Locker's field of concentration, which was to the right. I was monitoring the rest of the formation. The rogue plane now had my full attention. As I watched, unbelieving, it continued its nightmarish slide toward us. At this point I decided it was too much of a threat to be tolerated any longer. So I took the controls out of Locker's hands and executed a diving turn to the left, which took us below the intruding plane and into empty air space well below the formation.

Perhaps 20 or 30 seconds had elapsed since I had become aware of the vagrant B-17. By this time, I thought that all of the pilots and copilots in the threatened planes would have seen the danger and scattered, to reform when conditions stabilized. Again, not so. Sarten was looking up and in front to the lead plane just a few feet away. His copilot, who sat in the right seat, apparently could not see the path above and to the left that the rogue plane was following.

Then, it was too late. The rogue drifted through the place our plane had just vacated and swept across the backbone of the Sarten plane. Its belly sheared off the fin-and-rudder of the Sarten plane, just as it began to dive out of the way, and sent the whole assembly whirling back in the slipstream.

The rudderless Sarten plane immediately started down in a flat spin. I could not follow it very far because my view was primarily forward and up. We all wondered then and later why the crippled plane could not stay airborne, or at least go down under control. However, the fin-and-rudder assembly on a B-17 is its most prominent feature and contributes importantly to the plane's proper weight distribution and aerodynamics. It is also possible that the plane at fault did other damage that was not visible from the outside. For example, its propellers may have cut control cables inside the fuselage of Sarten's plane. In any case, the damaged plane could no longer remain aloft.

No parachutes appeared from the Sarten plane as it started down, but it had a long way to go before it reached the ground. Reports years later stated that the crew did get out but that several perished at the hands of their German civilian captors. This case served as an example of the practical caution that being captured by enemy military personnel was preferable to falling into the hands of civilians. The civilians had no reason to keep prisoners, and every good reason to dispose of them. How would German civilians feed prisoners, and why should they use up scarce resources on them? Killing is what wars are all about.

The rogue plane, although damaged on its underside, returned safely to England. I never heard anything further about the incident, but the plane's crew continued to fly missions. They were shot down a month later while returning from a mission to Merseburg, and crash-landed in Belgium (by then liberated territory) but suffered no serious casualties. Their faulty flying in the formation at Zeitz was simply a glitch that could have happened to any pilot under the pressure of combat formation flying. Disciplinary actions after the fact would have accomplished nothing. Grounding the crew would only have reduced available flying personnel. The very fact of the accident was punishment enough for the pilots who were responsible for the tragedy.

The flak at Zeitz was intense and accurate. Several planes suffered severe battle damage, but none was shot down. We did not learn what had happened to the rogue plane until we returned to Knettishall. Then we found out that it had returned ahead of us, and that the crew had reported that our plane was the collision victim! They had every reason to think so since we were closer to them than the Sarten plane had been just before the accident.

A few days after the Zeitz mission headquarters informed us that we had three-day passes to go wherever we pleased and to do whatever we wanted. We all packed our musette bags, which were canvas tote bags carried over the shoulder, and headed for London. The usual method was to get a GI truck to Thetford, which was about five miles away, and then take a train to London. I cannot remember any time that we had to wait unduly for a train, and I always enjoyed the trip. The train went through Cambridge and many other towns, then through the outskirts of London before arriving at Victoria Street Station. A three-day pass was always welcome because it guaranteed that we would be free from combat flying for at least 72 hours.

On my first trip to London I enjoyed all the sights and sounds of this picturesque city. I visited the Tower of London, ate fish and chips, and learned to like the scotch ale that a British officer introduced me to in the Piccadilly Hotel bar at Piccadilly Circus. (British drinks were not "warm" as often reported. They were "cellar temperature"—supposedly 55°, but not often iced.) I marveled at English institutions under the stress of war. It was a fascinating place. Black markets flourished. Women and soldiers were everywhere. I heard the chimes of Big Ben and saw the Houses of Parliament from The Embankment. The bells, however, did not peal out that Dick Timberlake would someday be Lord Mayor of London. Their ring might instead have foretold a very unpleasant event that would occur just one week hence.

Our three-day passes ended, as must all good things, and we were back at our base on 22 August. On 24 August 1944, we were wakened and briefed for a mission to bomb another synthetic oil plant near Brux, Czechoslovakia, which like Zeitz was near Leipzig. Most of Germany's synthetic oil plants seemed to be in this area because of the proximity to the coal fields from which the synthetic oil was derived. However, on this day our "bombs" contained propaganda leaflets instead of explosives. The message on the leaflets advised German civilians that further resistance was futile and urged them to give up.

We formed in the usual manner, and crossed the North Sea toward Germany. The weather was completely clear with visibility unlimited. We approached the target from the west. The flak was the closest and the heaviest we had seen to date. On most missions the roar of the engines drowned out exterior sounds. However, the flak was so close at Brux that we could hear the crashing of the shell bursts as they exploded with an ugly red flash and boiling black smoke. Each of us wore 24 pounds of armored flak vest and a flak helmet. This protection was certainly comforting and surely helped. Nonetheless, I recall at Brux getting a sharp feeling of insecurity for the first time. No longer was I watching all this action from a seat in a movie theater. Now I was in it, and jerking and cringing as the flak popped around us. One plane in our formation was practically blown out of the sky. All the rest of us returned to our base with much battle damage to our planes, several wounded airmen, and everyone wondering how we could survive 20 or 30 more such episodes.

Typical flak over a well-defended German target

Flak was an awful ordeal. It was so very visible and looked so deadly, as indeed it was. Most of the flak guns were 88 millimeter, which meant that the flak shell was about 3½ inches in diameter. Since the shells took 25 to 30 seconds to reach the proximity of their targets—our planes, at altitudes of 25,000 to 30,000 feet, we could evade them by making changes in altitude or direction oftener than every 25 seconds. This kind of evasive action would leave the shells bursting harmlessly to the side or behind us. However, at the Initial Point (IP) where we turned onto the bomb run leading into the target area, we had to fly straight and level. The lead bombardier needed a few minutes to make the adjustments to the lead plane's direction, such that the trajectory of the bombs would carry them to the intended target. So, on the bomb run we could take no evasive action, and our speed seemed agonizingly slow. From the ground a B-17 at 25,000 feet doing 180mph ground speed seems hardly to move at all. Bomber formations just seemed to hang there, often painting the sky with long white streaks—the condensation (con) trails from their engines.

After the turn onto the bomb run, our existence became a roulette game. Of course, the flak bursts that we could see were, by the very fact of their visibility, harmless. Their threat was what they foretold that was still to come. The moment bombs were "away," all planes in the formation would immediately bank and dive 1,000 feet like a school of fish. This maneuver put the flak behind and above us.

Although terrifying, the total damage the flak did to our formations was minimal for the Air Force as a whole. However, each plane was not a fractional "Air Force as a whole" that would suffer marginal damage. Direct hits by flak totally destroyed some planes and crews, even though perhaps 95 to 97 per cent of the planes on a routine mission returned to their bases. On every mission each of us could imagine that our plane was destined to be in the ill-fated three-to-five per cent. Data collected much later reported that enemy flak during 1944 destroyed more than 3,500 American planes, or six hundred more than fell to enemy fighters.

Upon our return to our quarters after the Brux mission, we learned that bomber command had scheduled another mission for the next day. A flag over the bar of the Officers' Club signaled this fact. If the flag was red, a mission was scheduled. If yellow, maybe and maybe not depending on the weather, logistics, and other factors. A green flag meant no combat mission.

Sure enough, the sergeant, whose duty it was to awaken crews, roused us out around 0530 hours. We dressed and went to the mess hall for breakfast, and then to the mission briefing room. The S-2 (Intelligence) Officer, as was customary, pulled back the cloth cover revealing a large map of Germany. Thumb-tacked ribbons charting our route showed us leaving the coast of England, following the North Sea northeast to the Jutland region, crossing the Denmark peninsula to the Baltic Sea, then turning south. Our target was yet another synthetic oil refinery near a town that was then called Politz, and just 10 miles north of the city of Stettin. We would be north and east of Berlin. (This area is now near the western boundary of Poland. What was Politz is now Police, and what was Stettin is now Szczecin.) Our penetration was about as deep as B-17s could venture from England to deliver a payload and expect to return.

We took off around 0700 in a plane named "Jake's Jerks." Ceiling and visibility were unlimited (CAVU). Since our trip was at least nine hours, we formed into our chain of bomber groups fairly quickly and did most of our assembly en route over the North Sea. We climbed at 150 feet a minute, and at 150 mph, indicated air speed. Ahead of us and behind us, as far as the eye could see, were groups of B-17s on their way to the target.

The day was 25 August 1944, and our pilot's birthday. On this account, our bombardier, Jack Moss, brought along his camera and took photos of the pilot and me from the navigator's astral Plexiglas bubble just in front of the pilots' windshield.

Around 1300 hours, we turned south from the Baltic Sea at a point near the mouth of the Oder River, and followed the river to the target. The IP at which we started the bomb run was east of Politz, so we were heading west to bomb the target.

The flak was again very heavy, very accurate, and very noisy. Spent bursts made a thunderhead of flak that filled the sky. The density of bursts suggested that a very large number of flak guns, probably several hundred, protected this target.

The pilot was flying the plane, following our element leader and concentrating on the proximity of other B-17s. I was monitoring the rest of the formation and the vital statistics of the engines by means of various gauges, most of which were on the copilot's side of the cockpit.

One moment I was sitting there, a normal unassuming 22-year-old American guy, not wanting to hurt anyone, but getting very uneasy about what was going on. I knew by this time that heavy bombardment was in the Big Leagues of Mars. In a moment I hoped, the newsreel would end, and we would all go outside and buy some popcorn.

I had it wrong. In the moment I might have tasted the popcorn, my right leg went numb from hip to toes. A giant had just hit my leg with a baseball bat. Immediately I thought, How bad is the wound? I cried out hysterically into my oxygen mask fearing the worst. I had no sharp pain, just an awful numbness.

The bomb run ended with "bombs away," and we made our usual diving turn out of the flak. I reached my hand down to my right thigh where the flak had hit me. Not surprisingly, blood stained my hand. However, the amount was minimal. I turned and showed my hand to the pilot. He was on the radio circuit for the formation, while I was on the "local" plane intercom so that I could talk with the crew. At this moment, with an anticipatory tingle and much to my relief, feeling came back into my leg. I could move my toes and bend my knee normally, though my thigh felt stiff and somewhat swollen. The bleeding also had almost stopped.

I pressed the intercom button on my flying control half-wheel and announced to the crew that I had been hit. A piece of flak had also hit the ball turret gunner, John Coco, in the foot, but the flak had not penetrated his flying boot. By this time we were well out of the flak barrage and beginning the long haul back to England. The navigator, Gene Finucane, came up from the nose to help me control any bleeding, but bleeding was not much of a problem.

I soon realized that my wound was not serious. A piece of flak about the size of a .32 caliber bullet had punctured the plane's aluminum skin and then hit the outside of my right leg. It was small enough not to have done major damage to my leg, even though, I found out later, it had penetrated well into my thigh muscle. Some aluminum detritus from the skin of the plane had also gone in with the flak. Since I had no broken bones and little bleeding, I was not in any immediate danger. I had no more discomfort than if my leg had been severely bruised in a game of football.

Nevertheless, we had a long way to go to get home; we were at least three hours from England. I decided to stay where I was in the copilot's seat. I knew I could still fly the plane if we had any further enemy actions that might incapacitate the pilot. Moreover, no other place in the plane was going to be any more comfortable. My oxygen equipment was working well, and I had my flak suit and helmet, my headphones, and my senses. No use upsetting a now stable equilibrium that would probably stay that way.

Locker had flown the plane most of the way in, and had counted on me to fly much of the way home, since it was his birthday. Occasionally, he gave me the controls so he could rest, but he did most of the flying for the nine hours and ten minutes we were in the air.

After what seemed interminable hours flying southwest over the North Sea into the sun, the coast of England came into view. Our group leader, according to convention, called the control tower at our base for landing instructions.

"Hello, Mecul," the call went. "Vampire Yellow, five miles out. Landing instructions, please." "Mecul" was the code name for the operational control tower of the 388th Bomb Group, and "Vampire Yellow" was the code name for our group.

"Land on runway 27 [from east to west]," Mecul responded.

In a few minutes our three squadrons of B-17s came over the field at 1,000 feet headed west, and began peeling off to circle and land at thirty-second intervals. The intense flak at Politz had downed two of our planes, so we were thirty-four instead of thirty-six.

On this 25th day of August 1944, however, our

plane and one other, according to the protocol that planes with wounded on board land first, peeled off and came in ahead of the others. As we made our approach to land, the engineer stationed behind the pilot and me fired red flares out of the special flare gun mounted on his turret. These flares signaled, "wounded on board." We made a normal landing and rolled to a stop where a base ambulance met us. I eased myself out of my copilot's seat, leaving behind my parachute, oxygen mask, helmet, and flak armor. Then I crawled down the passageway to the forward escape hatch, and let myself down onto a stretcher held by medical corpsmen. They loaded me into an ambulance and whisked me off to the Army's 65th General Hospital near Diss, about 20 miles from our base. I did not even take off any of my sheep-lined flying clothes.

When we arrived at the hospital after a ride of about 20 minutes, I received immediate attention. Doctors examined my leg and took X-rays. An anesthesiologist administered Sodium Pentothal in one of my arms—my first experience with that blessed substance. A nurse told me to start counting, but of course I comfortably blanked out without knowing that I was going.

I woke up the next morning in an officers' ward. Most of my fellows had combat wounds, and many of them were from the ground forces. Several had been wounded in France and brought back to England to recover before being returned to their units or sent back to the United States. A few others had non-combatant maladies, such as hernias, hemorrhoids, or infections.

My wound was well attended, but I never saw the piece of flak. The custom was to wrap the missile that wounded the soldier in a piece of gauze and put it on his bedside table. Somehow, the medical personnel who dug the flak out of me seemed to have misplaced it or had accidentally disposed of it. So I did not have it, and therefore did not know exactly what had hit me.

One of the surgeons, who had worked on me, told me when he visited the ward that they had had some difficulty cleaning out all the aluminum fragments that had piggybacked into my leg with the flak. In attempting to get them all out, they had cut a lot of inches on my right leg above and below the point the flak had entered, and also a separate incision on the back of my leg. I noticed that he seemed vague, and almost apologetic, about some details of the procedure. He did not know what had happened to the flak fragment, nor did any of the nurses or hospital orderlies. [For more on this puzzle, see page 198 below.]

I decided not to write my parents about my wound to spare them the mental agony of my very real danger. I thought that if I did not give them any particulars I might be able to gloss over the fact that I had become a statistic. So on my first day in the hospital I wrote a "normal" letter home, trying to sound newsy but not letting on that anything had happened to me. However, someone must have told me that such a ploy would not work because the War Department was required to provide the facts to close relatives of casualties. So I wrote them again the next day, explaining as best I could that I was not seriously hurt and not to worry.

Sure enough, on 12 September 1944, my parents received a telegram from the Adjutant General's office in Washington:

> DEEPLY REGRET TO INFORM YOU THAT YOUR SON SECOND LIEUTENANT RICHARD H TIMBERLAKE JR WAS SLIGHTLY WOUNDED IN ACTION OVER GERMANY TWENTY FIVE AGUST [sic] PERIOD PROGRESS REPORTS WILL BE FORWARDED AS RECEIVED.
>
> J A ULIO THE ADJUTANT GENERAL=

By the time this telegram reached my parents on 12 September, the event was more than two weeks old. In fact, my stay at the hospital ended on 11 September, one day before the telegram came to them telling of my wound. However, the AJ's office made up for that. They sent another telegram on 28 September saying:

> AM PLEASED TO INFORM YOU YOUR SON SECOND LIEUTENANT RICHARD H TIMBERLAKE JR RETURNED TO DUTY ELEVEN SEPTEMBER.

Maybe the War Department was "pleased" that I had returned to duty but I was devastated, no matter what I told my parents. War had become an inescapable and terrifying reality. I had had much more than enough, but I knew that I would have to go back on flying status unless the war (unbelievably) ended. Why me, I thought? I am only two-and-twenty, to paraphrase A.E. Housman, and much too young to die. I had not even begun to live.

The author recuperating at the 65th General Hospital, early September 1944

I would gladly have spent an unlimited amount of time in the hospital recovering. The weather was sunny and warm—late August and early September. The food was good; I was ambulatory; I had books to read; and I had comrades to talk to.

The stories I heard from my fellow patients denied that Allied forces were overwhelming the enemy with superior weapons and strategies. "We" were winning because "we" had greater quantities of everything. Through attrition, say, three of our tanks for two of theirs, "we" were grinding out a "victory," but it was not there yet.

The same day that I was wounded, Patton's forces broke through the German defenses at St. Lo in the Cherbourg peninsula and out onto the plain toward Paris, central France, and the German border. This news was all good. If only the war would end with this breakthrough! I listened intently to the news reports, feeling poignantly for the lives that were being lost on both sides, hoping desperately that the war would end.

Then, the unbelievable happened. With enemy forces in full retreat, Patton's tanks *ran out of gas* near the French-German border! The German armies then had a chance to regroup and reorganize their defenses. What a debacle of misallocated resources! With the gas that 1,500 B-17s used on one mission—approximately 3,000,000 gallons, Patton's tanks with Bradley's armies could have ended the war in the next few weeks. Where were the Services of Supply when we needed them? Had it been their tails that were on the line, Patton would have had his gas. But the breakthrough stalled at the German border, and the war lasted nine more hellish months.

Chapter 9: My October Missions With the Voertman Crew

Every morning that we did not have a mission and were hovering somewhere between sleeping and waking, we would often hear at a distance the sound of engines being tested on the flight line. Outside our barracks the mists of morning would shroud the landscape. Then, the base tannoy system's speakers would click on, and a gentle, unassuming voice would announce:

"Attention all personnel: In fifteen seconds it will be zero seven hundred hours. Five, four, three, two, one, zero seven hundred hours."

After this almost apologetic reminder that it was morning and seven o'clock—nothing. And nothing was precisely what we wanted.

When the Allied advance stalled at the Siegfried line, I stalled, too. Nonetheless, I recovered physically and could not deny the fact. So I returned to Knettishall and reported for duty. I had a few more weeks of recuperation, with heat treatments for my leg at the base infirmary. I am sure they did some good, but what I needed was for the war to be over. It just would not end. I watched the missions go out, and I shuddered.

On the morning of 17 September 1944 around 0900 hours, we were surprised to see another mission developing over us. However, it was not bombers that had formed and were heading east, it was formations of C-46s and C-47s towing gliders loaded with paratroopers. All of us on the ground quickly realized that something big was happening. We found out later that we were witnessing the American-British effort to breach the northern flank of the German armies by an air invasion of Holland. The planes we saw going over at about 4,000 feet were headed for Arnhem and surrounding territory. Several hours later, we saw them coming back. I remember distinctly a C-47 with about four feet of one wing bent up 90° from the normal horizontal, but still flying. However, the aerial invasion of Arnhem and Nijmegen failed, and many brave paratroopers lost their lives. (See the book, *A Bridge Too Far.*)

I was given a week's leave during the last week in September. I could have spent the time at a designated center for 'rest and recuperation.' Instead, I went to London and tried to prepare myself for the ordeal ahead. How was I going to force myself into the copilot's seat again? I bummed around London. All my senses seemed more acute. I was aware of every waking moment and treasured each one. The

American Red Cross had arranged to administer several hostels for the U.S. armed forces, so staying in London was comfortable. In addition, they provided some social programs that were very welcome.

One evening, Saturday 30 September, I went to a dance at The Reindeer Club in central London sponsored by the Red Cross. There I met Patricia Hart. She and I became good friends, and her companionship was especially helpful to me in my combat ordeal. My friendship with her, however, is another story, and one I shall never write for many reasons. It is sufficient that she knows how much I valued then and value now the support she gave me.

While I was in London, the V-1 and V-2 "buzz bombs" were an ongoing threat. I witnessed a few of the V-1 missiles over London before they shut off and came down to explode. I also experienced the concussions of a few V-2s at a distance. These missiles did not seem very threatening, probably because the German technicians at the launching sites had not aimed them at me personally. Of course, the V-bombs did much random damage and were a constant threat to Londoners.

Inevitably, my leave ended and I had to face the reality of a return to duty. So I boarded a train at Liverpool Street Station on 2 October 1944 and returned to Knettishall.

I had not flown at all for six weeks, including the entire month of September. This welcome respite was supposed to provide me "rest and rehabilitation," but I was far from rehabilitated. Nonetheless, I was back on active duty and had to cope as best I could with what lay ahead.

Immediately upon my return, another copilot friend of mine, Bob Voertman, who had just been checked out as a first pilot, asked me to join his crew as copilot. The crew's original first pilot had gone to a lead crew, so Bob, the copilot, had applied for the job of first pilot. Now he needed a copilot to fill his old position. By this time my original crew had another copilot, and I felt that my return to that crew would somehow be out-of-sync with their tour. I also felt that a change would help me with my personal struggle to overcome my apprehension at flying combat missions again. So I decided to make the change.

This new crew, which was now the "Voertman crew," had been in training with us in Florida. The pilot and navigator were particularly good friends of mine. So joining this crew was not opening up a Pandora's Box of uncertainties for me. The crew included, besides the pilot: Joe Rosenbaum, navigator; Ed ("Algie") Henderson, who was doing a second tour as a bombardier; Sydney Clark, engineer; William Wells, radio operator; Masil ("Shorty") Coughlin, ball turret gunner; George ("Doc") Yoder, armorer; and Robert Casper, tail gunner. Doc Yoder, at age 30, was the oldest member of the crew. Two of the gunners were in their 'teens, and the pilot and I were 21 and 22 years old.

The Big News I learned when I returned from London was that a synthetic oil plant near a town called Merseburg, and just south of Leipzig, had become "the worst target in Germany." The other two crews that had been with us all the way from Drew Field, the Lord crew and the Michaels crew, had both gone down on a nightmarish mission to this target on 28 September, just a few days before I returned from London. The Lord plane was the victim of a midair collision just after the bomb drop. Another plane in the formation doing a diving turn out of the flak struck it from above cutting it in half. By that time, flak had already seriously wounded the men in the nose of the plane. All but two of the crew (we found out later) perished.

Michaels's crew was more fortunate. Their plane, hit by flak after the target, could not stay airborne. However, the pilots, Michael and Waickus, controlled the plane well enough to ensure a successful bail-out. All the crewmembers survived the descent; all became prisoners of war; and all eventually returned to the United States.

This news was very upsetting. Not only did we know personally the men who had been lost, but also a new lethal target had come into our perspective: Merseburg. Besides the losses of the two planes whose crews we knew well, flak destroyed four other planes in the 388th Bomb Group on that mission.

Flak had become the Germans' weapon of necessity against Eighth Air Force bombers. The Luftwaffe had been defeated, not because its pilots and planes were inferior but because they did not have the fuel to wage effective combat. Flak defenses, however, had become more formidable. Intelligence had it that 1,000 flak guns defended targets in the Merseburg area. For other targets, our intelligence staff at mission briefings would often assure us, "There are only 10 (or 12 or 50) flak guns at the target." When we arrived at these targets, however, we would see the sky filled with spent flak bursts for miles in three dimensions. Obviously, the raw data our S-2 staff culled from their sources was somewhat faulty, but after the disastrous mission of 28 September it began to get some realism.

News of the Merseburg mission greeted me the evening I returned from London and the day before I started flying. In the next few days my new crew and I flew practice missions. Then, on the morning of 7 October, wake-up orderlies aroused us for a real mission—for this 22-year-old lad the acid test of whether I could again handle a flight into combat.

At the briefing room, we found that the mission was to bomb a synthetic oil plant at Bohlen, only a few miles from Merseburg. We were briefed as usual on the routes we were to follow in and out, our location in the bomber chain, and the anticipated weather. Again, as usual, the S-2 intelligence unit that briefed us understated the number of flak guns we would encounter at the target. Naturally, we did not find out that fact until later, and it really did not make much difference. We had to go through the flak no matter how many guns there were.

Take-off was at 0700 hours. We climbed through the overcast in the conventional manner, assembled at 18,500 feet, and proceeded toward southeastern Germany. About 20 minutes before we reached the IP, our bombardier, Algie Henderson, called our attention to a group of fighter planes about two miles away at eleven o'clock, level. Henderson had finished a 30-mission tour several months earlier, and had witnessed enemy fighter attacks several times. "Those aren't ours," he stated flatly. His words chilled us, especially me. I did not even have a popgun to ward them off.

The enemy fighters, we could now determine, were a conglomerate of 30 to 50 ME-109s and FW-190s. They snap-rolled and cavorted as we watched. Then suddenly they were on the attack, not at us, but at the group directly in front of us, the 452nd Bomb Group. The distance between our two bomb groups was two to three miles, but all of us looking forward from our positions had a newsreel view of what occurred, and it was not a scene calculated to inspire peace of mind.

The German fighters pressed in driving through the 452nd Bomb Group formations, then coming back around to attack again. B-17s laboriously pulled out of their clusters, some with engines on fire, but all beginning a last descent to earth five miles below. Then, just as suddenly, our P-51 fighter escorts counter-attacked the German fighters, and the dogfights continued below where I could not see them. In a matter of a few minutes (at most) the fighters had appeared, had attacked, had left their calling cards, and had paid the admission fee. One or two ME-109s came near us, but they were on their way back to their bases and had no resources left to attack us.

When the news first crackled through our group that enemy fighters were approaching, the formation closed up like a fist. Every pilot understood that our strength was in our concentrated firepower, and that in turn depended on the tightness of our formation. Twelve B-17s in a tight squadron formation had 72 .50-caliber machine guns facing forward. More important, German fighter pilots chose the loosest formations for their attacks. If they saw a tight formation, they would look for others that seemed less professional or even sloppy.

We still had the target to contend with. Cloud cover was about eight-tenths, so our bombardiers used their Mickeys to aim their bombs.

Nothing much happened at the target. If we could not see them because of the clouds, neither could they see us to aim their flak. So, when the cloud cover was extensive, the bombing was often inaccurate and the flak was correspondingly less lethal. Our return trip was uneventful, and we landed at our base in the middle of the afternoon. For the 452nd it was another story. They lost close to a dozen planes that day.

To me this mission was a personal victory. I had put my butt back up there to get shot at, and had managed to endure the test. On this mission and every mission thereafter, I experienced a strange elation just as we made the diving turn off the target after "bombs away." Somehow, for that brief moment I felt invincible. Unfortunately, that feeling did not last very long. By evening the sickening feeling of dread had returned.

I flew only three more combat missions during October. On 9 October we went to Mainz. Cloud cover was complete, so we saw nothing except clouds and some inaccurate flak at the target.

October 13 was a Friday, and for those who are superstitious it lived up to its reputation. Several of us were sitting around in our barracks that evening listening to a Master Sergeant's stories about squadron personalities, and just gossiping. Suddenly the base tannoy system outside our barracks blared out, "Air raid alert: Yellow!" We noted the warning, but continued to talk without taking any precautions.

A few minutes later, another alarm sounded. This time the warning color was "Red," emphasizing that some kind of German aircraft or missile was in our neighborhood. We stopped talking and listened. Finally, the tannoy shouted, "Air raid alert, Purple," which meant that something was almost on top of us.

Then we heard it—a V-1 buzz-bomb with its peculiar staccato exhaust, and it sounded as though it was coming in the door! Some of us, I included, foolishly tried to get out the door before the bomb came in. The others ducked under beds. Just as I exited the barracks, the "thing" went directly over us at an altitude of less than 200 feet. But instead of shutting off and dropping down to explode as was their mode, this one just kept on going . . . and going . . . and going, and within 20 seconds was out of sight over western East Anglia. We watched for a few minutes, but no explosion . . . nothing. It had to come down somewhere, but it was out of our sight when it did. One possibility is that it failed to explode when it dropped, but more likely it was just out of our range. It taught us one thing: When the air raid alert says, "Red," do not wait for it to get "Purple." Get to the bunker immediately! The air raid bunker was a semi-cylindrical steel framework banked up with much earth, and very close to our barracks. It was effective protection, but except for this incident I never had occasion to use it.

A German JU-88, a very capable twin-engine medium bomber, had launched this missile from somewhere over the North Sea. The V-1 buzz bombs that came into the London area were launched from the Dutch or Belgium coast, and later from the German coast. However, all of the buzz bombs that came into East Anglia, aimed at the bomber bases, were air-to-ground missiles from JU-88s.

On 17 October we were sent to Cologne to bomb the marshaling yards. Flak was moderate-to-intense even with clouds. We bombed from 27,000 feet, and lost one plane.

Shortly after the Cologne mission, about October 19 or 20, I woke up in the early morning with an acute pain in my neck. It was so bad I could hardly move. On hearing my distress, my bunkmate friends helped get me up and over to the infirmary. I had no other symptoms and I had no inkling of what caused my problem. For about five days I was incapacitated. The flight surgeon gave me aspirin and other pain killers, but only time provided any cure. For the next several days, the only thing I could "fly" was the Link Trainer. Meanwhile, my crew flew two missions without me.

I have it in my flight record that I "flew" the Link Trainer three times that week. The Link Trainer was the WW II version of what is now called a flight simulator. Our Link Trainers, however, did not simulate any particular plane. They were solely to improve a pilot's familiarity with instruments and his flight performance in overcast weather.

On 28 October 1944, the Squadron Commander provided me the opportunity to get checked out as a first pilot. Accordingly, I put my mind into high gear and reported to the flight line for the test. I sat in the pilot's seat on the left, and Captain Poland, an experienced lead pilot, sat in the copilot's seat. By this time I had eight missions and 540 total flying hours, so I was thoroughly familiar with the flight procedures of the B-17. All that remained was to show that I knew how to fly the plane from the left seat.

Captain Poland was a fine officer, and he inspired confidence in me. We had only a skeleton crew as our flight plan was simple: Take off, fly the traffic pattern perhaps exiting it once or twice, then reenter the traffic pattern and land. I did all the flying.

I was unused to having the throttle controls in my right hand and the flight control wheel in my left, the reverse of the hands' position in the copilot's seat. However, I adjusted with only one minor difficulty. Every time we landed, Poland would tell me to open the throttles and take off again. Upon his order I would walk the throttles forward, but I sometimes neglected to roll some down-elevator into the elevator trim tab at the same time. Consequently, the control wheel would tend to come back into our laps as the engine power went on. Then, I would correct properly for the renewed thrust.

A few minor glitches aside, the results of my test flight were very good. I shot 22 landings that day in the first pilot's seat, without any critical mistakes in procedures or mechanics. This test duly qualified me as a first pilot.

The next day the command officers in the squadron offered me the opportunity to be a first pilot with my own crew. After only slight deliberation, however, I turned down their proposal. Everyone's overwhelming goal was survival. My present crew, I knew, counted on me, and had a better chance of surviving with me as copilot. I, too, had a better chance of surviving with them than with a new crew and the associated uncertainties I might encounter. So I thanked the squadron commander and replied that I would stay where I was for the time being.

Two days later, 30 October, we were briefed for another mission to Merseburg. We dressed and prepared for the mission despite the fact that the weather was extremely unfavorable. We took off around 0800 hours, and climbed an hour and a half on instruments at our usual 150 feet per minute to assemble at 14,500 feet.

I cannot recall all the details of how we managed these impossible formations in that very soupy English weather. On a typical mission-day, 1,200 to 1,400 four-engine bombers would take off from about 25 airfields, and climb around designated courses that were strictly demarcated for each group. When we reached an altitude above the cloud cover, we would coalesce into group formations. Lead planes that had taken off first would gather their flocks together by firing flares periodically as they made an elliptical pattern around two radio signals. Our lead planes usually fired red-green flares, and we had no difficulty finding them. Then, we would link up group after group in a chain two hours long (at 180 ground miles per hour). The final formation into a bomber stream or chain would often take place en route to the target, but always at an altitude where the air was clear. We sometimes climbed twenty thousand feet through clouds, but we always had to have a clear space at some altitude to position ourselves in formations. Thus, assembling the bomber formations and positioning the many bomber groups was an exacting and tedious procedure. Fully one-third of our mission time was spent on this phase, much of it over England.

The sight and, especially, the sound of those 1,200-plus four-engine bomber formations from the ground was awesome beyond description. No one who has ever seen and heard that particular resonance will ever forget it. The sound was not loud in the sense that one needed ear plugs to prevent tinnitus. It was not deafening. It was simply a pervasive, inescapable, low-pitched throb that completely filled the whole environment for hours on end.

The waste and destruction of capital were appalling even without accidents, and of course accidents happened. Every so often an airfield below us would show a telltale plume of black smoke where a loaded bomber had lost some vital function and crashed on take-off. I often reviewed what I would do if one of our engines quit just as we were getting airborne: Turn up the supercharger control knob from "8" to the maximum "10," lower the flaps 20 degrees, jettison the bomb load by means of a toggle switch on my dash panel, and that would be it. Fortunately, I never had to use my last resort procedure. Our Wright Cyclone engines never faltered, and neither of my pilots ever tried to pull the B-17 off before it was ready to fly.

On this day, we proceeded routinely out over the North Sea toward Holland where we would cross the front lines into Germany. Our flight plan had us going in at 27,000 feet, an altitude that was supposed to take us over the cloud tops of the current weather front. When we reached this altitude over Holland, however, the clouds still in front of us towered much higher than 27,000 feet. We could not fly over them.

Above 28,000 feet, air pressure is so reduced that oxygen by itself is not enough to maintain human efficiency. Auxiliary air pressure, which we now experience on every commercial airliner without ever knowing it, is required at high altitude to get the oxygen into one's lungs. B-17s were not pressurized—an understatement. (The new B-29s were internally pressurized, but they were never used in the European Theater.) So with the air pressure reduced to less than three pounds per square inch—from 14.7 pounds at sea level, we could go no higher than our present altitude for the time it would take to complete this mission.

Our mission that day, therefore, became a mission impossible. For any such event, rare as it might be, we had in our daily flight plan a "recall phrase"—one that every American airman would recognize. It was always some universal platitude, a slang word or slogan, such as "Sultan of Swat," or an advertising line, such as "Breakfast of Champions," the one for Wheaties breakfast cereal.

On this day as we approached the weather front that towered to the east, we heard over our intercoms the welcome recall, "Pennsylvania Quakers." I might say that there was much rejoicing as we saw all the formations in front of us now turning 180° and heading back to England. Nobody wanted to go to Merseburg, nor to any other target for that matter, but especially not to Merseburg. Our group formation duly made its 180-degree turn and followed the crowd back to England. We landed around 1330 hours in the afternoon.

The question at our critique after this partial mission was: "Are we going to get credit for this one? Is it going to count toward our tour?" The answer to this question depended on how far east toward the target we had gone before we turned around. As luck would have it, we had been seven-plus degrees east of Greenwich, England, so the effort did count as a mission. We had also flown for six hours and forty minutes, which was longer than the total flying time on some complete missions.

Some unfinished business, however, remained.

Chapter 10: Missions in November 1944

"Pennsylvania Quakers" brought us back on 30 October. However, the synthetic oil plant at Merseburg was still there, so we were certain that our reprieve would not last long. Sure enough, three days later, on 2 November 1944, bomber command again scheduled us to go to Little M. (Since Berlin was "Big B," Merseburg should certainly have been "Little M." No one except bomber crews of the 1944 era ever heard of it, but it was a more formidable target in terms of flak than Big B.)

This mission to Little M was my first to this notorious target, even though I had been to Bohlen and Zeitz, which were near by. It turned out to be momentous for many reasons. We took off around 0800 hours and followed the usual course into the heart of Germany. The weather again was difficult but not impossible. Stratus cloud formations appeared at several altitudes, but no imposing weather fronts intervened.

As we approached the target area, a shock wave of alarm resounded through the bomber formations: Enemy fighters were seen in the area, *and they were jets*! About that moment I saw one—the first non-propeller aircraft I had ever seen, several thousand feet below us and coming up from two o'clock at an unbelievable angle.

The plane, however, was not a jet. It had a rocket engine, and was a Messerschmitt 163 "Komet." [I wrote a letter about the incident to my brother George a few days later, and penned a small top view of the plane's profile. My letter stated that it was a ME-163, and my drawing shows only one engine and no stabilizer assembly. These details confirmed that it was not the better known ME-262, which was a conventional jet aircraft with two jet engines. I still have this letter.]

All the gunners waited tensely as the ME-163 approached. Around to the back of our formation he went and out of my sight. Then he came in from the rear, but he was attacking another formation of B-17s somewhere behind us. I felt our plane vibrate as our gunners tried some long distance 50-calibre deterrents. The pilot of the rocket plane, however, did not press his attack decisively. I do not even believe he fired his guns, if indeed he had any to fire. I saw no tracers or other evidence of weapons in use. However, by this time he was behind and below my view of things.

Something else was strange about this whole affair: Our fighter escorts were nowhere to be seen. Where were they? What were they waiting for? Were we supposed to send them engraved invitations to come to the party?

We found out later that the Luftwaffe Command had sent up eight to twelve ME-163s as bait. They were to lure our fighter escorts away from the First Air Division B-17s behind us, so that a goodly number of their conventional fighters—ME-109s and FW-190s—could attack the groups following. However, our fighter command somehow figured it out, so they let us deal with the ME-163s, which were largely for dramatic effect anyway. The Komet had a very restricted range because of its limited fuel supply, and many other problems. No one reported any damage from these sham attacks. However, the First Division B-17 formations behind us had one of the biggest aerial battles of the war with the conventional ME-109s and FW-190s.

We approached the target area and turned north at the IP to begin our bomb run on the notorious Leuna synthetic oil plant. The flak was heavy and accurate.

Then, we noticed, a glitch had occurred in the sequence of our formations. We were no longer in a front-to-rear bomber chain. The chain had somehow become kinked so that we were side-by-side with another group on what was supposed to be the bomb run.

As I looked out to my right at the group beside us that should not have been there, one plane veered away from that formation with its left inboard engine (no #2) on fire. For a minute or so it held altitude as the pilots tried to contain the fire. Then it started a gradual spiral and disappeared below. It never blew up within the time it was visible to us. It just went down.

Since we were side-by-side with another formation, we could not make a normal bomb release and a diving turn out of the flak to the Return Point (RP). Our awkward position forced us to hold onto our bombs, and to detour several miles off course. Instead of turning out of the flak, we were forced to stay in it . . . and in it . . . and in it—for 25 minutes. Normally, we were in flak only from two to five minutes. But on this day we would no more put one barrage behind us than another series of bursts would pop up in front. Six bursts would often appear simultaneously, in a stepladder sequence of roily black puffs. It was like a nightmare in which we had to endure a continuous menace . . . and could never wake up. Our bombs finally fell in the northeast corner of Leipzig, which was more than 20 miles from Merseburg! Nevertheless, we endured. All of our planes, somewhat the worse for wear, returned to our base at Knettishall by 1600 hours.

Three days later on 5 November 1944 orderlies woke us for a mission to bomb in front of advancing ground troops near Aachen. Admittedly, this kind of tactical support was hard on the ground troops but it was "milk run" stuff for us. Enemy fighters were almost non-existent at such times. Also, the flak was usually thin and inaccurate because the major flak concentrations were kept for the defense of strategic targets, especially those manufacturing synthetic oil.

Yes, we were supposed to bomb in front of the troops advancing around Aachen. However, there was one proviso: If the weather was not clear enough for bombardiers to be absolutely certain of their tactical targets in front of the ground forces, we were to pull off and bomb a secondary target. The secondary target was the synthetic oil refinery at Ludwigshaven on the Rhine River.

Well, as bad luck would have it, the skies over the lines near Aachen were too cloudy to bomb tactically. So the formation leaders called off that sally and led us toward our secondary target at Ludwigshaven. Again as bad luck would have it, the weather at Ludwigshaven was clear as crystal with visibility unlimited.

We went in over the target at 27,000 feet. The flak was horrendous—intense, accurate, and both "barrage" and "tracking." German flak gunners threw up a huge bundle of flak at each formation as it went over, and also tracked the formations going in from the IP. One of our planes, piloted by Lieutenant Thurman Esselmeyer, suffered a flak burst right between the copilot and the right inboard (#3) engine and went down. We found out years later that the copilot, whose name was Pure, was killed instantly. However, the other crewmembers, including the pilot, bailed out and became German prisoners of war.

Our plane did not get away without some travail. When we were on the bomb run, flak pieces damaged some of the electrical circuits that controlled the bomb release mechanism. Consequently, when the bombardier in the nose of the ship hit his toggle switch to release the bombs and reported, "Bombs away," the radio operator immediately shouted, "They didn't go; they didn't go." Half the bombs, all in the rack on one side of the bomb bay, did not exit.

One of the radio operator's jobs was to monitor the bomb release. From his position in the radio room, he had an easy view into the bomb bay, and could report any hang-up of the bombs. When I heard him cry that the bombs "didn't go," I also tried to toggle them with a switch I had for that purpose on the dash panel in front of me. But that switch also was ineffective, so the only way to release the bombs was to do it mechanically.

The bombardier then called the armorer, who was also a waist gunner, to see if he could release them. To do so, Doc Yoder, the armorer, had to walk out on the catwalk in the bomb bay. The catwalk was a heavy steel beam, and part of the backbone of the ship. Hand rails along the sides provided support to anyone walking through the bay. Once in the bomb bay, Doc could easily reach the bomb release "dogs" and jettison the bombs by actuating their release mechanisms with a screwdriver.

We were now out of the worst flak and stabilized, but still above 20,000 feet. Undaunted, Doc attached a portable oxygen bottle to his oxygen mask and got out on the catwalk to release the bombs. In his excitement, he also took off his flak suit before he went into the bomb bay! So there he was five miles above Germany, with a torrent of-40° air rushing around him, some flak still popping, and no flak suit. Doc released the bombs one by one with his screwdriver and got back into the waist through the radio room without further incident. The bombardier then closed the bomb bay doors. Fortunately, nothing more added to our present difficulties.

Doc explained later that the thought had gone through his mind that if he accidentally dropped his flak suit, the quartermaster would have billed him for it on a "statement of charges." So he took his armor off before venturing into the bomb bay! Doc's thinking was an example of the strange notions that one may conceive under pressure.

The flak severely damaged many other planes, including ours. However, we were back to our base and landed by 1430 hours in the afternoon. This mission was my second to Ludwigshaven, and both had been calamitous.

The next day, 6 November 1944, we were called for a practice gunnery mission. We took off in the late morning, climbed to 10,000 feet and rendezvoused with a P-47 fighter somewhere away from any population centers. The P-47 then made passing attacks at us, and our gunners practiced firing back with camera "guns." After about 30 minutes of this simulated attack, the P-47 made a close-in pass, slow-rolled in front of us, and signaled "goodbye."

After the fighter left, we had nothing to do but return to our base. However, I casually recalled a theoretical operating procedure that Voertman and I had occasionally discussed. "Now might be a good time," I suggested over the intercom, "to see how this thing operates with all four engines feathered."

Voertman was entirely sympathetic to the idea, and we prepared for the event. Not only would we get experience with the B-17's feathering procedure, we could measure with some degree of accuracy how far a B-17 would fly as a "glider." He and I knew, I should add, that the engines gave the plane thrust and the wings gave it lift. We were not about to see how it flew without wings. However, some members of our crew were not all that sophisticated.

With our interest and anticipation of such a venture in high gear, we began the procedures for feathering engines: Put the propellers in "high" pitch, nearest the fully feathered position; switch off the generators; shut off the fuel supplies; pull back the throttle levers. Finally, push the red feathering buttons on the dash for engines 1, 2, 3, 4, and switch off the two magnetos that provide spark to ignite the fuel-air mixture in each engine.

The engines and propellers, in sequence, slowed and stopped with all the props turned edgewise into the wind, i.e., fully feathered. As the number 4 engine rotated to a stop, the sudden silence became deafening. I then called the crew over the plane's intercom. "Look," I said facetiously, "no hands." The pilot had the plane in a steady glide downward at 125 miles per hour, which was supposed to be the most efficient speed for descent. We observed our rate of descent, and later calculated that from 25,000 feet we could glide close to 80 miles before reaching the ground.

Having done our homework, we prepared to restart the engines. I opened the fuel cocks. The pilot adjusted the propeller controls for low pitch, switched on the magnetos, and opened the throttles. Then, I energized the flywheel for the number 1 engine. When we tried to engage the flywheel to turn the engine, it acted as if it did not want to start. It had quickly chilled down due to the low temperature at altitude.

The pilot then tried an alternative tactic. He pulled out the feathering button for that engine to undo the feather, so that the propeller would unfeather and start the engine turning. The procedure was much like that for an automobile with a battery too weak to turn the starter. The driver puts the car in gear with the clutch disengaged and coasts down a hill. (There must be a hill, of course.) When the car has enough momentum, the driver lets out the clutch. The revolving rear wheels turn the drive shaft, which, through the transmission, rotates the engine so that it starts functioning on its own. This sequence simply reverses normal operating procedures: Instead of the engine starting and subsequently furnishing power to the wheels, the turning wheels start the engine, and it then assumes its normal role of supplying power.

Our "hill" was the 8,000-or-so feet of altitude we had left after our gliding experiment. However, a problem had developed. The propeller on the number 1 engine did not want to come unfeathered. For a few brief seconds we thought we might be in deep trouble. However, the pilot crossed the controls of the ailerons and rudder. That is, he banked the plane to the left while pushing right rudder so that the plane would slip to the left. This maneuver put enough oblique force on the propeller to start it turning. Finally, it sputtered into life, a very welcome sound. Once the first engine was turning, we had plenty of electric power from its generator to start the other engines.

Back in the waist section of the plane, however, an alarmist scenario had developed. One gunner, not of our crew but a visitor who had come along to get in his required gunnery training, had panicked. Not understanding that engines do not hold the plane up, he had presumed when he saw the stationary props and stilled engines that we were due to crash. He thereupon jettisoned the side entry hatch in the rear waist section of the plane, had his hand on his parachute ripcord, and was ready to bail out! Apparently he had also convinced two or three other members of the crew that we were in deadly peril, and they, too, were ready to shout, "Geronimo!" and abandon ship. However, some wiser and cooler heads calmed down the jittery gunners and no one jumped.

When the pilot and I got wind of what was going on back in the waist, we realized that we should have explained more clearly what we had planned. Since we had discussed our procedure over the intercom, we thought other crewmembers had heard and understood what we were doing. It never occurred to us in our 22-year-old wisdom that anyone would think that stopped props and engines constituted an immediately perilous predicament. Even if we could not restart the engines, we would have been able to land in any one of at least five airfields. As it was, everything stabilized, and we landed back at our base without further incident. We did have to explain why we were missing the rear hatch door.

Our companion flying officers were interested to learn of the powerless glide information we had obtained from our experiment. But otherwise, we heard nothing more about the incident. As far as I know, no one had ever tried our experiment before or did so afterward. It just may not have had enough scientific merit for further study.

Our next mission on 9 November was to bomb the marshaling yards at Saarbrucken. We took off just after 0600 hours, and assembled at 18,000 feet. The target was not very far into Germany. We were there by 1000 hours and bombed from 23,000 feet. The flak was accurate, but cloud cover below us reduced its effectiveness. Nonetheless, two B-17s in our group were missing.

This mission saw the end of our flights with sheepskin flying clothes to protect us from the cold. On this day, we had cloud formations both below and above. The high cloud above us was thin, but it filtered out so much sun that the cockpit did not receive its usual warming. The "greenhouse effect" from the sun's radiant energy was missing. Consequently, the pilot and I became chilled to the bone even though we were decked out in all the sheepskin we could wear. Fortunately, we had an electrically heated muff that the pilot had brought on board. Using this device, we could keep our hands warm. The one flying the plane had to have both hands free for the controls, and the one 'off duty' had both hands in the muff. Fifteen minutes later, roles were reversed. The temperature outside was less than-40°.

This muff, though a boon, was not enough. Our feet, even in sheepskin flying boots, got colder and colder in spite of our most energetic efforts to maintain circulation. By the time we landed at our base about 1300 hours, the big toe on my right foot was slightly frostbitten. So I went to the infirmary, and was detained there for the night, though the frostbite proved to be temporary.

About midnight an ongoing commotion awakened me. A mental patient in the infirmary had become violent. Medical orderlies restrained him and forced him into a straitjacket. I was too tired to stay awake and ask about details even if I had wanted to. I believe that this was the familiar case of a man having taken more combat than he could bear. Many of us were probably at the edge of this same abyss, and were just barely holding on.

My pilot, Bob Voertman, and navigator, Joe Rosenbaum, showed up at the infirmary early the next morning to inform me that we were now on a three-day pass and should get a move on. Usually, Air Corps administrators granted a three-day pass the day before it was to begin, so that those so privileged could get a half-day head start. But this time we had not been so blessed, and therefore had no time to lose. I quickly secured my release from the infirmary. We then hurriedly packed our musette bags, got a GI truck ride to Thetford, and were ready for the next train to London. We were in London for the next three days—November 9, 10, and 11.

The weather was cold and rainy throughout this period. When we returned from London, it was no better. Nonetheless, we were briefed for another tactical support mission on 16 November to bomb in front of our troops who were again attacking the German forces near Aachen.

We took off around 0800 hours. The flight was uneventful, and the weather while not perfect was clear enough to bomb as briefed. So we bombed from 23,000 feet in front of those poor guys on the ground and hoped for the best.

Our real problems started when we returned to the air space over England . A dense fog had come in over East Anglia, and getting hundreds of B-17s back into their home fields had become impossible. Most groups, therefore, were diverted to other bases. Our group was advised to land at a Royal Air Force base near Bristol, which was about 130 miles west of our base at Knettishall.

It was no trick to get there; the problem was to descend through the overcast. We had a formula for doing so. The procedure required a steady descent, flying a racetrack pattern around two "bunchers," as they were called. A buncher was simply a device that sent a radio signal we could hear in our earphones. Sometimes we would have to come down through 15,000 feet of clouds before we could see the ground. Preparing to descend from above the clouds, we would head in the proper direction, then "peel off" one after the other above the cloud bank as if we were going to land. Instead of landing on ground, we "landed" on cloud. We would enter the cloudbank at say, thirty-second intervals at 160-mph air speed, and descend at some precise rate—usually 500 feet a minute. This kind of procedure demanded that all pilots keep their air speed and rate-of-descent uniform to avoid tragic collisions.

Our descent to the RAF base near Bristol proved uneventful. After we landed, our ships were dispersed appropriately and we had a chance to hobnob with our English brethren.

The first planes I saw there were RAF Spitfires. Some of them had four-and five-bladed propellers, instead of the conventional three-bladed ones. I supposed these planes were part of some kind of aeronautical experiment. I watched one Spitfire taxi near us on the flight line and come to a stop. The hatch opened and the pilot who emerged was unmistakably a woman. I learned then from some British ground crew that women pilots—WAFS—were flying noncombatant duty—ferrying Spitfires and other British aircraft. How I envied that lady! How I wished I might fly Spitfires! (No, no don't ask. Don't even think about it. Just try to survive.)

Day followed day at the British base, and the weather stayed rainy, foggy, cold, and unflyable. To me it was a welcome respite. I would just as soon have stayed there for a month. But after three days of impossible weather, we were cleared to take off for our home base. It did not look any better that day as far as I could tell, but we were told to go ahead. (Maybe our British hosts did not have enough supplies to keep us any longer.)

So we prepared to take off. I asked the pilot to

let me do the honors, and he obliged. I went through the normal pre-flight procedure, got a green light from the tower, and walked the four throttle handles forward to full power: 46 inches of manifold pressure and 2500 rpm. Not having much of a load, our plane readily picked up speed. When it reached 110 mph, it lifted off. However,I held the nose down so it would pick up more speed, and more. At 100 feet off the ground and maybe 140-mph, I banked it over and chandelled into the mist. Nothing too exciting, I just wanted to leave our Limey friends in style.

To get back to Knettishall without climbing above the overcast to a high altitude, we had to stay below three hundred feet. We did so all the way back. I recall the field at Knettishalll showing up on that gloomy day, the rows of runway lights finally appearing as the only bright feature in that entire dismal gray world.

The mission to Aachen on 16 November had been my thirteenth. On 30 November, two weeks later, we were briefed to bomb a synthetic oil plant at Lutzkendorf, another small town in the Leipzig area, and also near Merseburg.

The evening before this mission, as Voertman and I had been walking home from the Officers' Club, we noticed that heavy clouds were rolling across the sky. I suggested that it looked like a warm front was coming in and we would not fly the next day. However, wake-up orderlies rousted us out around 0600 the next morning. As we shivered along to the mess hall before the briefing, we noticed the sky was now clear. I suggested that the apparent warm front coming in the evening before must have been "a warm front aloft." My pilot and navigator good-naturedly pooh-poohed my sophistry. However, when the meteorologists briefed us on the weather for the mission, they commented that "a warm front aloft had passed through the area during the night." I glanced at my friends, who had rather sheepish looks on their faces, and humbly reminded them of my observation.

The taped lines drawn on the mission map showed the routes we would follow in and out. Since Lutzkendorf was in the vicinity of Merseburg, the same thousand flak guns would defend it that defended Merseburg. On the formation sequence board, which showed B-17-silhouettes of groups and their places in the bomber stream, the 388th Bomb Group was nowhere to be seen—until we looked at the very end of the formation placements. And there we were, the last group in the Third Air Division of the Eighth Air Force that would go over the target. We all sensed then that this mission did not look promising for our longevity.

Our takeoffs began at 0845 hours. The weather was CAVU (ceiling and visibility unlimited) all the way in and all the way back. This "effort," the official word used to describe the magnitude of the bombing force, featured 1,200 bombers escorted by 1,000 fighters. We are talking here about logistics. The bombers alone required 3¼ million gallons of 100-octane gasoline.

Our group got to the target area about 1300 hours. The first groups had been there over an hour earlier. In fact, so many planes had gone along the same route at approximately the same altitude that our bombardiers had to aim their bombs "through dense and persistent contrails," as the official report put it. We were at 28,000 feet. Besides the contrails from hundreds of B-17s, smoke screens and the smoke from previous bombs obscured the ground.

The flak was heavy and accurate. Our group missed the assigned target and bombed an electric power plant five miles away.

Con trails on mission to Merseburg

When I thought about this mission afterwards, I realized that our tail-end position in the bomber stream might have improved our chances. By the time we arrived at the target, the flak gunners may have used up much of their available ammunition. The bombs could have damaged them, too. While the flak guns defending strategic targets were not near the target proper but rather dispersed some miles around it, many of the bombs that missed their targets must have damaged or destroyed some of the flak guns. In the event, we did not lose a single plane. Many of the planes had serious battle damage, and one tail gunner whom I did not know was killed. Enemy fighters were conspicuous by their absence.

Next day, the headline in the Stars and Stripes, the U.S. Army's official newspaper, featured the headline: "Fifty-Six Heavy Bombers Lost." Such losses were of the magnitude of losses in the early missions to Regensberg and Schweinfurt. Those missions, however, had fewer planes participating—three to four hundred, so their losses were relatively much worse. In addition, the loss statistics on this mission were somewhat biased, because many of the "lost" planes landed as cripples in Allied territory and were not properly accounted for until a day or two later. On the earlier missions planes that went down short of England were gone forever because the Allies held no territory in Europe. Nonetheless, by any criterion Lutzkendorf was a dreadful mission.

Chapter 11: Missions and Activities in December 1944

Our next mission to Mainz on 4 December served as an example of just how far "pin-point" bombing could miss. We were to bomb the marshaling yards at Mainz from 24,500 feet. However, clouds covered nine-tenths of the sky at the target, so the lead bombardier used his Mickey to "aim" the lead ship's bombs. As the lead ship defecated, all the other bombardiers toggled out their turds, too. The flak was meager and inaccurate, but the bombs missed their target by 11 miles. We returned to our base around four o'clock in the afternoon having accomplished next to nothing.

A welcome respite occurred at this point. On 6 December command headquarters granted our crew a seven-day leave at what airmen called the "flak shack." The Eighth Air Force had at least half a dozen of these rest-and-recuperation havens for bomber crews and fighter pilots. Officers and enlisted men went to different locations, but they were all similar in quality and method of operation.

The other three officers of my crew and I went to Aylesfield House, a magnificent country home that a wealthy Englishman had built in the 1930s. He leased it during the war either to the British government, who made it available for Eighth Air Force use, or to the Air Force directly. (I have looked in all my reference books on the Eighth Air Force and have not found one mention of the flak shacks, much less any detailed account of their operations.)

On 8 December 1944, I wrote my parents describing our flak shack: "[Aylesfield House] . . . is a beautiful mansion about an hour's train ride [south and west] of London. All our [needs] are taken care of. We get to sleep as long as we want in nice soft beds with real sheets on them, and we get very good food. Also, we have all the recreational facilities you can think of with Red Cross hostesses to help us enjoy them. . . . They also give us civilian clothes to wear during the day. The House is the kind you read about in books . . . It's in the middle of a large estate and has beautiful grounds surrounding. There are about 25 of us [flying officers] here."

Although sleeping late was an option, we were always awakened in the early morning by an accomplished English butler, who was appropriately clothed in black formal garb. He knocked and then entered our room with a tray of fruit juices. "Juice, sir?" he would ask politely. Then, he would peel back the drapes from the large window overlooking the fields around and exclaim: "Oh what a beautiful day, sir! I am sure you will enjoy it."

The day might be miserably gray, overcast, and raining, but he was right. Any day I woke up in that place with those surroundings and the ambience of Aylesfield House was "a beautiful day." The butler was a prop, of course, to make us feel welcome and relaxed. He could not have been cast better for the part, or a more authentic representative of what was solidly British.

Our day was completely free to do with as we pleased, even leave for some hours to go into London. If we stayed around the House, we could entertain ourselves with card games, Ping-Pong, hikes in the country, and, most memorably, horseback riding.

Aylesfield House had its own stable with ten to fifteen riding horses. Of course, such a herd required a stable master to manage and care for the horses. This man also provided instruction and guidance on riding. Good that he did, because those of us who chose horseback riding as one of our day's activities sorely needed his assistance. Decked out in casual civilian clothes provided by the House staff, we would assemble near the stable. Then, under the supervision of the stable master we would get horse-borne and ride single-file out into the lanes and country roads of the area.

I had never ridden horseback before, but I twice volunteered to try it while at Aylesfield House. Without flak in the offing, nothing else seemed very risky. So one gray wintry morning I found myself high atop a relatively docile steed. I tried to practice what I had observed from watching others in this precarious position. I had the reins in my hand and thought that they controlled the horse. Pull up and he should stop. Put pressure on the left rein and he should turn left, and so forth—similar to the controls on a B-17.

In fact, none of these common means of control had any effect on my horse. The stable master, who was proficient in this art, controlled his mount perfectly, as he led us through the countryside. Most of the time the horses walked. But occasionally the stable master would put his horse into a trot or a gallop for a short distance. When he did so, all the other horses would do exactly what the lead horse did. I had no control over my horse at all. He knew who was boss, and the boss's name was not Lieutenant Richard H. Timberlake, Jr.

Nonetheless, the ride required concentration and gave the rider some exercise and a sense of achievement. So it was fun—with one exception: The roads were muddy and looked slippery, especially for horses' hooves that had no "sure-grip" on their shoes. To make matters worse, my horse seemed to have stumbleitis. When he started to gallop following the stable master's cue, he would misfire slightly every so often as though he was losing his footing. The slippery mud and his stumbling gait led me to expect that the nag would go sprawling at any instant. So every motion faster than a walk put me on ready-alert for a soft place to land if this no-control horse went down forcing me to bail out. Fortunately, it never happened.

One other horse, I noticed, kept kicking up his hind hooves, as if to repel something behind him that he did not like. I thought at the time that his skittishness might endanger the horse and rider behind him. I found out two months later, when I was again in the hospital, that this occasional kickback finally found a mark: one of his hooves broke the tibia of a flying officer riding the horse behind. Flak was not the danger at the flak shack; it was horses and hooves!

Fighter pilots also visited the flak shack for rest and recuperation, so we had interesting discussions with our fighter escort comrades. One fighter pilot there was Charles ("Chuck") Weaver of the 357th Fighter Group, who had trained with me in Primary and Basic flight training. During his combat career, he was credited with destroying 11 enemy planes. We had a grand time together exchanging experiences. We could not anticipate then that we would lose touch after the War, but meet again 52 years later as "Old Boys."

Every evening we reverted to our forest green dress uniforms, and had supper served by the butler and his helpers in the beautiful dining room. We talked shop a lot to let off steam, although everyone was careful not to let off too much. Then there was after-dinner dancing and relaxation. The week was such an oasis in the desert of war that it could only pass too quickly.

We returned to our base at Knettishall on 13 December 1944. I had completed only 15 missions in the four months since August 11—less than half my required tour of 35 missions, and I could see no light at the end of the tunnel. The rest of my crew was six missions "ahead" of me.

Our next mission was to bomb the marshaling yards at Hanover on 15 December, and it was uneventful. The 388th formation again was the last group in the bomber chain over the target. We bombed from 24,000 feet through a complete overcast, and returned to our base by 1530 hours. Flak was meager and inaccurate.

This period of the war around mid-December 1944 suddenly became serious and threatening because of the breakthrough of the German armies into Belgium. Von Runstedt's forces drove back Allied armies even though U.S. defenses held near the Belgium town of Bastogne. The salient of German armies into Belgium became "The Battle of the Bulge."

Coincidentally, beginning about 16 December, our East Anglian air bases began to experience thick, persistent, freezing fogs. Yes, freezing fogs! Morning after morning, fog came in from over the North Sea then froze, sometimes half-an-inch thick, on everything. Often, it was very beautiful, but it practically grounded the heavy bombardment program. The fog was more of a problem than the ice. After the mission to Hanover on 15 December, we did not fly another mission until 24 December.

The author posing in B-17, and holding puppy, with ice from freezing fog in the background, near mid-December 1944

We had one interesting aside. One day near 20 December, we were alerted in the middle of the morning to report to the flight line for a mission. We hurried to comply, and were getting into our flying clothes in the equipment building where we suited up. Before we could get any further, we had word that the flight strategists had scrubbed the mission. Rumor had it that Eighth Air Force command had seriously considered sending heavy bombers in at low level to carry out tactical operations against the German armies in the Bulge. Such a consideration showed how serious the German offensive had become. It surely would not have been a very healthy action for us. B-17s and B-24s were just too vulnerable down low, as the tragic and disastrous low-level mission to Ploesti a year or so earlier had demonstrated.

Our mission on 24 December 1944 was the largest military air action in history. Nothing like it was possible before World War II, and the circumstances for a repeat could never occur again. Modern war technology does not require such massive inefficient use of such clumsy machinery.

The target for our group that day was an aircraft base near Darmstadt. The official take-off time was 8:40. At that hour near the winter solstice in central England, the sky is barely light.

Every plane in the Eighth Air Force that would fly that day was airborne. Some did not have guns, and some did not even have bombs. The idea was to present to the Germans the specter of an invincible and overwhelming armada of air power. Instead of the usual 24 or 36 bombers, our group command put up 71 bombers! Other groups did likewise. The final tally was more than 2,000 heavy bombers, 1,000 fighter escorts, and some thousands of medium bombers, light bombers and fighter-bombers.

Of course, all these aircraft required an ocean of gasoline and huge amounts of materials and ground support to get them in the air. Once in the air, the bombers had to form into strategic chains of bomb groups so that the sky was not a helter-skelter chaos of planes banging into each other. Forming took many hours. Our path to the target area, according to our navigator, "took us on a Cooke's Tour of Germany" so that all the bomber formations could be fitted into the effort.

The winter sky was clear for a change, so we could see the ground and the gunners on the ground could see us. As we passed over the front lines on the way in, flak bursts suddenly appeared. Not being on the bomb run, we could take evasive action to avoid the flak. However, our group did not get away scot-free: a burst crippled one of the engines on the lead ship causing it to abandon the mission. The command pilot on this plane was Lieutenant Colonel Chester Cox, who at the mission briefing had enjoined us to get our bombs on the target—or somewhere in Germany, no matter what. In fact, our lead ship was leading not only our group but also all the other groups in the 45th Combat Wing. The deputy leader then took over the lead.

My pilot and I took turns flying formation—on and off every 15 minutes. And let me note here that flying formation is exhausting and tedious work. It has no glamour in the air, no matter how pretty it looks from the ground. The pilot flying has to monitor precisely and consistently the plane he is following in the formation, and make constant small adjustments with both engine power and flight controls to keep his plane's relative position fixed.

After interminable hours flying formation, we reached the target area and bombed from 25,000 feet. The flak at the target was moderate and accurate, but all our ships returned to England. We landed at Knettishall just at dusk. So, on this day, we took off before dawn and landed after sunset, approximately 9½ hours later.

We did not see any enemy aircraft over Germany. However, as we approached our home base to land, the word went out for all planes to keep the .50-caliber gun turrets manned because enemy fighters were attacking returning formations over East Anglia! After we landed, we found out that a number of German Focke-Wulf fighters had surreptitiously followed some of our bombers back to England. They had attacked while the bombers were in the landing pattern, and had shot down three or four bombers—I think B-24s. Talk about nerve! It was like something out of a book where the outnumbered "good guys" make a brilliant sally against the forces of evil. Only, we were the good guys. . . . Weren't we?

Altogether, 24 December 1944 was a strange and unforgettable day. Besides all the other things that happened, German fighters shot down one of the lead planes in a group piloted by Air Force Brigadier-General, Frederick Castle. For his actions in this engagement, Castle was awarded the Congressional Medal of Honor. He was the last airman in Europe to receive this award during World War II.

As we landed in the gloom, we were alerted to the fact that we would be flying another mission the next day—Christmas. Sure enough, orderlies awakened us Christmas morning, and we got as far as the briefing room before the mission was scrubbed. Again, it was the freezy-foggy weather, but everyone was relieved not to fly that day.

The goal of strategic bombing continued to be an attempt to blunt the German offensive that had started 16 December. Allied forces had to turn the tide in the Battle of the Bulge before they could make further progress on any front. Consequently, German airfields and railroad marshaling yards were the targets of choice. In line with this objective, our next mission on 28 December was to bomb the marshaling yards at Koblenz on the Rhine River. We took off around 0915 hours, and saw bombs away through an undercast at 1300 hours from 25,000 feet. The flak at the target was minimal.

Again, on 30 December we were briefed for a marshaling yard at Kassel, which is just about in the middle of Germany. This day our group was leading the Third Air Division, so we would be the first planes over the target. Not only would our group lead, but, in addition, six planes including ours would pull out ahead of our lead formation. Our special job was to drop down about two thousand feet and throw out extra chaff that we carried in place of bombs in order to jam German flak guns.

Chaff consisted of aluminum foil strips, perhaps 12 to 18 inches long and ¼-inch wide. Typically, the radio operator stuffed the chaff out of a chute in the radio room during the bomb run. The chaff fluttering slowly down was supposed to form a metallic cloud that would diffuse the sighting of the flak radar below us during the bomb run. On this day since our plane was dumping extra chaff, other gunners helped the radio operator with this task. (I do not remember now, but it is possible that they threw the chaff out of other openings besides the chute for that purpose in the radio room.) Since the air was clear, the ground gunners five miles below could see us anyway, chaff or no chaff, but at least they were frustrated in one dimension. The official report described the flak as moderate and inaccurate, "... but ... quite accurate on the chaff ships. ... The chaff a/c [aircraft] did an excellent job of dispensing chaff in the target area." We were flak decoys that day and got away scot-free.

The next day, however, was not so scot-free. Our group, without our crew, went on a big mission to Hamburg. It turned out to be very rough. Two planes from our group were shot down and others had severe battle damage.

Thus ended 1944.

Chapter 12: Missions in January 1945

By this time I had completed 19 missions. Although my combat tour was more than half-finished, every mission still brought a sense of foreboding. One could not let himself think of what might happen, or what it might be like "to finish up." Just take every day as it comes; thinks only of each minute as it happens; sleep as much as possible; and prepare for each mission to the fullest. To paraphrase Mr. Samuel Johnson: Self-preservation in the presence of life-threatening hazards clears one's head remarkably.

On 5 January 1945 our group bombed the marshaling yards at Hanau near Frankfort-on-Main. After take-off at 0800, we climbed through clouds until we got to 22,000 feet, where we broke out into the clear and could assemble into formations. Climbing through clouds was a nerve-wracking job. We had to maintain 150 mph indicated airspeed, climbing 150 feet per minute—yes, 150 feet *per minute*, with superchargers boosting manifold pressure to 46 inches, and props turning 2500 rpm. We maintained a racetrack pattern around two radio signals while climbing. Each plane was one minute behind the one in front that had taken off one minute sooner. As long as everyone was doing the right thing, our speed and climb relative to each other would be zero or nearly zero, and collisions would not happen.

All B-17s in the Eighth Air Force had distinctive markings that identified their group affiliation. Since our planes were a part of the Third Air Division, each of our B-17s had a black square on its rudder and another black square on top of the right wing. In each square was a white letter "H" that identified our plane as one from the 388th Bomb Group. All B-17s in the Third Air Division had the black squares, but of course with different letters. The lower the number of the group, the higher in the alphabet was its letter. For example, the 100th Bomb Group had a white "D" on the tail and right wing of its planes. The First Air Division used triangles on the rudders and wings, and letters in the triangles to identify their group numbers. Most of the First Air Division bases were slightly west of Cambridge, which meant that they were fifty miles from the Third Air Division bases. All of the Second Air Division planes were B-24s.

I relate all this tedious information because of an incident that occurred on our climb through the overcast the day we went to Hanau. We were at about 18,000 feet, and climbing our lonesome way through the clouds, when suddenly a B-17 crossed our path not more than 200 feet in front of us and at our level. It was there-and-gone in an instant, and it had a triangle on the tail. Therefore, it was from a First Air Division base, and 50 miles from its own base assembly pattern!

I do not know that the sudden appearance of this stray B-17 shocked us. If not, it was only because its presence was so fleeting. Were others nearby? How had this glitch occurred, and how could it be avoided in the future? We still had the mission to deal with, so did not do much more than exclaim at the event. We immediately radioed our group leader and our base headquarters. Nothing more came of this near miss, but it revealed vividly how midair collisions could occur.

After forming at 22,000 feet, we climbed to 25,000 feet. Over the continent the skies were clear, so we bombed the target at Hanau visually. However, the contrails were so thick from all the planes' engines that we could not even see the group two minutes in front of us. The flak was again meager and inaccurate. We returned to our base around 1730 hours just as it was dark.

By this time of winter, the air at high altitude was always very cold and often very damp. Consequently, our engines were producing dense and persistent contrails on every mission. Each engine burning gasoline emits exhaust gases mainly of carbon dioxide and water vapor. The hot gaseous water vapor, exiting through turbo-superchargers and exhaust ports, quickly froze into ice crystals. Contrails close up appeared to be white spirals forming approximately fifty to one hundred feet behind each engine. Their presence marked our altitude, speed and direction most accurately, but did not add significantly to our flying difficulties. Sometimes, they were persistent enough, given other climatalogical conditions, to form an entire cloud cover where skies had previously been virtually clear.

The next day, 6 January, we flew yet another mission to Ludwigshaven. We took off at 0830 hours, climbed through overcast to 13,500 feet, and headed for Germany around 0930 hours. Clouds covered the target area completely, so the flak was not as deadly as it had been on our previous missions to Ludwigshaven. We bombed from 25,000 feet, and returned to our base by 1500 hours.

I now had 21 missions, a number that qualified me for promotion to first lieutenant. The manual on technical operations specified that pilots be promoted to first lieutenant after their sixth mission, and copilots, navigators and bombardiers after their 21st. So, sometime between 6 January and 10 January my promotion to first lieutenant came through from headquarters. No superior officer notified me; there was no ceremony; no band played the Air Corps Song. I came back one evening from the officers' club and a bombardier, who always knew everything that was going on, informed me from his bunk in our semi-darkened barracks: "Tim, you made 'first'." I thanked him, but I felt very little gratification—almost, 'So what?' The flak at the next target would not change just because I had become a first lieutenant.

On 13 January we flew again. The target this time was a marshaling yard at Bischofsheim, a town in central Germany near the junction of the Main and Rhine Rivers. We climbed to 13,000 feet through overcast, formed at 15,000, and bombed visually from 25,600 feet. The flak was moderate to intense, and accurate. It knocked the bombardier in the lead ship from his sight, and caused him to trip the "salvo" bomb switch accidentally. This switch releases all the bombs in a plane's bomb bay all at once—in a salvo. When the bombs from the lead ship dropped, all the other bombardiers toggled out their bombs, too, so the bomb results were "poor." On the return we went through high clouds that again promoted dense and persistent con trails from our engines. We also had to make another instrument descent through 10,000 feet of clouds when we arrived at our base around 1500 hours.

Two days later, 15 January, we were briefed for a mission to bomb the marshaling yards at Augsburg in extreme south central Germany. At times in the past, this target had been very tough. Because it was a long way into Germany and was an important rail center, enemy fighters frequently made an appearance and took their toll.

We took off just before 0800 hours and climbed through 12,000 feet of clouds before forming. When we arrived at the target around 1230 hours, cloud cover below us was 10/10s, or solid, so we bombed by radar. Somehow or other, the lead plane in the high group made an accidental release seven miles, or two-plus minutes, too soon. The flak was light and inaccurate—just about as effective as the bombing. We could see the Alps Mountains and lots of snow on the ground. Altogether, it was a grim and unpleasant day. We landed around 1600 hours. I now had 23 missions, not close to the end but getting there.

By chance one evening soon after, I met the base flight surgeon in the Officers' Club. He asked about our crew's tour and when we would be finished. I replied that the crew had six more missions to get to

35, but that I was six behind them, so had twelve more to do. At this point he very kindly informed me that I would probably finish officially when they finished. He noted that, because I had been wounded, Eighth Air Force Headquarters would forgive the remaining missions on my tour. I realized that he had the authority to initiate such a recommendation, and that he was telling me he would do so. The thought gave me fresh hope that I might make it through my tour after all. In effect, this very humane flight surgeon had just given me six missions.

Nevertheless, I still had several more to go no matter what the count. On 20 January we were briefed for a mission to bomb the marshaling yards at Rheine in northwest Germany, only a few miles east of the Dutch-German border. The most difficult part of the mission was the assembly, which required us to climb through overcast to 20,000 feet. From take-off to the break-through into the clear at 20,000 feet took two hours. All the marshaling yards we were bombing at this time were tactical targets in support of our ground forces, and not many miles from the front lines.

On this particular mission we ran into a frustrating and inexcusable predicament. We were low element lead of a three-plane Vee in the low squadron. We had not seen any flak or enemy fighters and were nearing the IP when our squadron leader began losing altitude. Down, down, down he took us in a flak area renowned for the accuracy of the flak gunners. No word came from the lead ship on what we were doing or why. When we were down to 21,000 feet, my pilot and I, after a short consultation, decided we had had enough. We turned our ship away from our position as low element lead, and, with our wingmen following, started climbing with full power toward the lead and high squadrons. By this time they were 5,000 or more feet above us. Nevertheless, we caught up to the lead group and bombed with them.

The excuse given after the mission for the unexplained descent was that some light flak received earlier had damaged one or two of the turbo superchargers on the lead ship's engines so that it could not maintain altitude. Given this circumstance, why did the command pilot take us all down toward perdition just because he could not maintain altitude? Every lead plane had a deputy lead right next to him, ready for just such an eventuality. My thought is, and was then, that the lead pilot simply did not want to go it alone. So he let us all follow him down to protect his butt! He should have called for fighters and let us continue with the deputy lead in charge.

No flak of any consequence appeared at the target. Bombs were away from 27,500 feet through 10/10s-cloud cover at 1017 hours in the morning. The bombardiers had to use their Mickeys to "aim." We were back to our base in East Anglia by 1230 hours.

My pilot and I discussed our pull-away from our squadron leader at the mission critique (now called a "debriefing"). I cannot recall any official reaction to our initiative. I think the group leader may have slapped our wrists with a noodle. What else could he do? Tell us he would not allow us to fly any more missions if we ever did that again?

Our move to abandon the formation appealed to me as a thinking individual. We had confronted an uncertainty in flight, made a decision based on the facts of the case, and carried out a deliberate response on our own. In later discussions of this incident with our friends, abandoning a formation "for cause" was labeled, "Joining the 21st Air Force," an entity that did not exist.

The next day, 21 January, we flew again. Our mission was to bomb the marshaling yards at Mannheim across the Rhine River from Ludwigshaven. This time our group again led the entire Third Air Division of perhaps 400 B-17s. We climbed through cloud cover to 21,000 feet before forming. Our engines again made dense, persistent contrails all the way into the target and back. We bombed from 27,000 feet. Flak at the target was moderate but accurate. Since the flak gunners could not see us visually, this mission was not nearly as costly as earlier ones to the Mannheim-Ludwigshaven area. One of our planes went down, but all personnel from it survived as prisoners-of-war.

We had now become "old" and experienced airmen who "knew what the score was." On most of our missions we led a Vee-element of three planes, which meant that we flew off the squadron lead in some dimension. Two other Vee-leads also flew off the squadron leader. While the 12 planes took up a fair amount of sky in a vertical dimension, the fore-and-aft dimension for the squadron was fairly short. This formation profile was designed to concentrate bombs on a given target, and to provide the best defense against fighter attacks.

The targets we visited in January were all tactical. The German breakthrough into Belgium was still a problem for our ground forces, and our missions sought to ease the pressure against them. That was still the idea for our next mission.

Chapter 13: Mission #26 to Hohenbudberg, 28 January 1945

On Sunday 28 January 1945, we were briefed to bomb a marshaling yard at Hohenbudberg, a small town in the Ruhr River valley just west of Duisburg, and east of Krefeld. This section is a complex of cities that compose the industrial center of Germany. None of us had ever heard of Hohenbudberg, and I only found it much later—with help from a friend—on a very detailed map of Germany. It apparently was nothing more than a large railroad yard with some supporting infrastructure.

Our target time was 1300 hours. We took off, climbed, and assembled in the usual manner at 21,000 feet, then followed our briefed route toward the target. We were not going deep into Germany, but the Ruhr valley was notorious for its intense and accurate flak. Eighth Air Force bombers almost never went into this area. Mostly, British bombers of the Royal Air Force—Lancasters and such—bombed targets in the Ruhr and at night to minimize exposure to flak.

Even as we took off and assembled, I felt something was different about this mission. One difference was that we were going into the Ruhr, and we had almost no combat flying experience in this area. Finally and unaccountably, I did not have the feeling of apprehension and dread that I had experienced on every mission since the previous August. Possibly, I felt more at ease because the target was insignificant enough to be considered a "milk run." Also, I knew we were getting close to the end of our tour and I may have let down my psychic defenses—just as a runner, anticipating the end of a race, slows down just before reaching the finish line. I did not like this feeling, because I knew I needed my guard up and my adrenaline working.

The weather was cloudy at different levels and with snow squalls here and there. My pilot and I took turns flying, turning the controls over to each other every 15 minutes, as was our custom. By the time we turned onto the IP around 1300 hours, I was flying. Since the air was very cold, perhaps 60° below zero, we experienced a lot of frosting inside the cockpit. The four throttle handles on the console between us were iced up and stuck together from the moisture our hands exuded through our gloves. The side windows and windshield inside the cockpit were also icing up from the water vapor given off by our breathing. We countered this problem by using the edges of a plastic container that held the mission details—codes, recall phrase, altitudes, etc.—as an ice scraper. Sometimes when we scraped, we made a veritable snowstorm in the cockpit.

My goggles were also frosting up. Since I was flying the bomb run and had to see clearly what was going on, I moved my goggles up over the top of my flak helmet. It was a trade off—visibility for eye protection, but necessary for a short while.

The flak on the bomb run was not particularly heavy, but it seemed uncomfortably accurate. Seemed and was. Suddenly, my windshield had a hole in it. A flak fragment, perhaps the size of a large caliber bullet, had glanced off the inch-thick glass, creating a fist-sized hole, and spraying glass fragments into our faces. My left eye felt some of these tiny pieces, just as though someone had thrown sand very hard into my eye. I was not at all blinded. I could still see with only slight discomfort, although the glass particles clouded the vision in that eye. The pilot had some scratches on his face, but his eyes were unaffected.

We quickly realized that no major damage had occurred in the cockpit other than to the windshield. I was still flying, looking out to my right at the plane I was patterning in the formation, when I noticed engine oil spewing out around the propeller hub of the number four (right outboard) engine. The oil was soaking the engine nacelle and spreading back over the wing. Almost simultaneously, Joe Rosenbaum, the navigator called on the interphone to warn me: "Look at that Number Four engine!" The uncontained oil served notice that flak had cut some oil lines, and that the engine would quickly become much more of a liability than an asset. "I got it," I responded, and reached forward to push the number four feathering button on the dash panel.

As I explained above when we feathered all four engines on a gunnery practice mission, the feathering buttons were a row of four, very red, very visible push-button switches in the middle of the dash panel. Either pilot could reach them easily. Once the propeller was feathered, all fuel lines and electrical circuits to the affected engine had also to be shut off so that the engine would not try to keep running.

Just as I pushed the number four feathering button, my left leg went numb from hip to toes. The force seemed identical to what had numbed my right leg five months earlier. It was as though pushing the feathering button had again set in motion the giant and his baseball bat. The shock crumpled me, and the pilot, seeing I had some distress, took over the controls.

The numbness in my leg prevented me from assessing how much damage the flak had done. I realized, however, that shutting down the crippled engine was still a priority. I did not want to be wounded, and also have to deal with a fire. So I quickly went through the rest of the feathering procedure—fuel switch: off, mixture control: fully leaned, turbo supercharger: off, number four prop pitch: high. It was not very difficult; I had practiced it innumerable times in my mind.

By this time the bombardier had toggled out the bombs. The number four engine was dead and its propeller fully feathered. I pressed my intercom button, which was under my right thumb on the control wheel, to tell the crew of my plight but no sound came forth. I could hear sound in my earphones, but could not project my voice.

To my great relief, tingling and feeling came back into my left leg. I found that I could move my toes and ankle. But when I tried to move my lower leg at the knee, the "knee" seemed to be in the wrong place. I could tell then that my thighbone (femur) was broken precisely in the middle. So I took off my oxygen mask and shouted this fact across to the pilot. The air was so thin at 26,000 feet that it would hardly carry my voice even those few feet, but the pilot heard me and relayed the information to the rest of the crew.

The piece that did the damage, I found out later, was about the size and shape of the first two joints of one of my middle fingers. It came up through the skid plate for the rudder control just behind my right foot. On passage it ripped through the back of my right flying boot scratching the skin behind the Achilles tendon, hit the steel control column, or "stick," gashing the steel five or six inches and cutting my intercom speaking wire as it did so. Finally, it ricocheted off the control column and into my leg breaking the femur. It stopped about two-thirds of the way through my leg.

When he understood my condition, the pilot informed the group leader that he had wounded on board, and that we were going to take a direct route back to England. Fortunately, we were not more than an hour or so from our base in East Anglia. So we abandoned the formation and headed home alone, nose down, with the remaining three good engines doing their job.

I was very concerned that I might be losing blood. I could not see the wound because it was on the nether side of my leg. From what I could see, however, I judged that my blood loss was minimal. The flak seemed not to have hit an artery nor seriously damaged major nerves. Flight engineer Sydney Clark tried to help me. However, he could do very little. He and the bombardier, Doc Yoder, saw to it that I was getting all the oxygen I could use. Then I had them help me shoot a vial of morphine from the emergency medical kit into my leg. I did not think at the time that it was a general narcotic; I simply assumed that I should inject it somewhere near the wound. Besides, we had cut away some of my flying suit so that my upper left leg was exposed. The flak, though it was still lodged in my leg, had made a bruise spot on the top of my thigh that showed where it would have come out. Moving to a different place in the aircraft was out of the question. I could not be moved anywhere, and I could never have exited the plane had it been on fire.

Our situation was now stabilized. We were going downhill back to England as fast as we could by the most direct route, probably making a ground speed of 200 mph. I looked at the instruments registering engine data, but my mind could no longer make sense of what they were telling me. Engine rpms, manifold pressures, oil temperatures—none of it made sense, except that the gauges for the dead number four engine were zero everything. I knew at least that those dials were telling me what I needed to know.

Unaccountably, the feathered propeller on the number four engine slowly started to unfeather itself, possibly because our airspeed was so high. As I watched, it gradually started windmilling. I tried to re-feather it to no avail. So it just went on windmilling all the way back, adding some unwanted vibrations as it did so.

In less than an hour—I would say, by 1400 hours, we were in voice contact with the control tower,

Mecul, at our base. When we approached the field preparatory to landing, however, local snow squalls had reduced visibility virtually to zero. The pilot banked around trying to find a hole that would allow us to get down, but nothing opened up. At one point as he banked to the left trying to find a clear spot, I felt that the plane was slipping dangerously because the dead engine on the right side was not producing any power. So I took the control wheel momentarily— the last time I would ever touch the controls of a B-17—and heaved it around to bring the plane back to level flight. The pilot accepted my correction, took over the controls, and ordered the navigator to direct us to another field.

Airfields, of course, were everywhere. One of the nearest was the base of the 100th Bomb Group at Thorpe Abbotts, about 20 miles east of Knettishall. The pilot made radio contact with that base, and in a few minutes we were in their air space and ready to land. Eighth Air Force legend had dubbed it, "The Bloody Hundredth," because on three different occasions, enemy fighters and flak had wiped out the whole Group to a plane.

So here we came on the approach to the landing runway, on a wintry, snow-squally afternoon, and my last landing ever in a B-17. Red flares arced out of our top turret as the engineer fired his flare gun alerting medical personnel that our plane had wounded on board. What could be more appropriate than to make a last landing, wounded and in a crippled plane, on a cold, gray, wet, afternoon at the base of the 100th Bomb Group! This scene had surely been played here many times before.

I do not remember much about the landing except that it seemed normal. I lowered the flaps on the approach, and after we touched down the brakes worked well. So no hydraulic systems were out. The powerless, windmilling engine on the starboard side caused no problems. As we lost speed after landing, it dejectedly stopped. Ground personnel directed us to taxi toward the ambulance area where medical help was available.

After the plane stopped and the remaining engines were shut down, a flight surgeon and two or three medics came on board to evacuate me. Before they could do so, however, they had to get enough access to my broken leg to immobilize it with splints. Then, they maneuvered me onto a stretcher that they positioned between the pilots' seats and down into the cramped access tunnel leading toward the nose. In this space was the forward access hatch. When these preparations were completed, the medics eased the stretcher with me on it through this opening.

Once on the ground, the base flight surgeon checked me again, and the medics then lifted me into the ambulance. I said my brief good-byes to the crew. We all knew that my combat tour was, perforce, finished. My mouth was terribly dry, partly because of dehydration and fever, and possibly because of the morphine.

The ride to the 65th General Army Hospital near Diss was uneventful. After x-rays and a quick diagnosis, I was in the operating room. I advised the doctors, who might have overlooked it, about the glass in my left eye. An anesthesiologist administered sodium pentothal, and later, I found out, a mixture of nitrous oxide and oxygen. For me the lights went out. My combat tour, my active military life, and my flying career were now a closed book.

Chapter 14: Recuperation in the 65th General Hospital

Western Union

WASHINGTON DC [FEB] 14 1032P[M]
RICHARD H TIMBERLAKE SR
731 NORTH FOURTH ST
STEUBENVILLE OHIO

REGRET TO INFORM YOU YOUR SON
FIRST LIEUTENANT RICHARD H
TIMBERLAKE JR WAS SERIOUSLY
WOUNDED IN ACTION TWENTY
EIGHT JANUARY IN [sic] GERMANY
MAIL ADDRESS FOLLOWS DIRECT
FROM HOSPITAL WITH DETAILS=
J A ULIO THE ADJUTANT GENERAL^

About twelve hours after hospital surgeons started working on me, I began to hover between sleeping and waking. My first coherent awareness that next morning, 29 January 1945, was of a hospital orderly trying to get me far enough awake so that I would take the sulfadiazine pills he was urging on me. Dutifully, I took the pills with water and, as soon as they were down, immediately chucked them right back up. Then, while the orderly was cleaning up the water and pills I had just swallowed and regurgitated, I went back to sleep. I had received some blood transfusions during the night, but nothing was going into my arm now. Gradually I gained full consciousness, and when I did I realized that I was very uncomfortable.

I was in an orthopedic bed and rigged up in skeletal traction. A supporting apparatus held my left leg up at a twenty-degree angle. A pin through my left shinbone just below the knee served as an anchor for a metal wishbone attached to both protruding ends of the pin. The wishbone in turn was attached to a single strand of rope that went to a pulley at the foot of the bed. The other end of the rope was fastened to a ten-pound weight that pulled my lower leg and the lower half of my broken femur toward the foot of the bed. On the other end, a harness under my left hip, attached by another rope to a pulley and weight behind the head of the bed, pulled the other part of my broken femur up and away from the lower part. The obvious strategy here was to prevent the muscles from pulling the leg together. If not for the traction, the leg would grow short when the bone knit.

The structure that held all this static machinery

was a framework of black iron pipes similar to construction scaffolding. I had a small trapeze on a chain above my head that I could use to pull myself up in bed. Both ends of the bed could be manually cranked up or down for a number of different purposes. However, the occupant of the bed could not do the cranking. For this function he was dependent on nurses, orderlies, or fellow patients.

I was in a Nissen-hut hospital ward. The hospital consisted of a number of these familiar structures linked together. Each section was half-cylindrical corrugated sheet metal with windows, and was about fifty feet long and twenty feet wide. A dozen beds were in rows along each side, and two coal-fired stoves kept the ward heated. Altogether, it was a comfortable, economical, and sturdy structure.

On this morning, however, I was very uncomfortable. My left leg did not hurt, but its placement in the traction apparatus limited my movements to such an extent that I ached from inactivity. In addition, I had a fever, I was nauseous, and my bandaged left eye interfered with my orientation. I was still terribly thirsty. After the sulfa episode, I asked the orderly for something to drink and he brought me a Pepsi-Cola. I managed to hold down the Pepsi, and it revived me considerably.

Gradually the ward woke up. Nurses brought around washbasins with warm water, wash cloths, and soap. The nurse who brought mine left it by my bed, so I proceeded to bathe myself as best I could. When she returned, she remarked that she had been planning to wash me and was surprised that I could do it myself.

Nurses brought breakfast, but I could hardly eat anything. On the day I was wounded, I had had some breakfast but nothing thereafter. So, by this morning I had not eaten for twenty-four hours. Even after my nausea tapered off some days later, all food looked and tasted like sawdust. I knew I had to eat something to repair my leg, so I tried to eat the tastiest foods they served. However, I was not succeeding. Consequently, the ward doctor prescribed something for me that would promote appetite. After I started taking this medicine, my appetite gradually got back to normal. For at least a week, however, my intake of nutrients was very much below par, and I lost some weight that I could ill afford to lose.

The discomfort of being rigged up in leg traction, my fever, the bright lights in the ward, the ongoing routine noise of the place, and the irritation in my left eye all combined to make me very unhappy. I ached for nighttime when the lights would be turned off and the ward would get quiet. Sleep I could and did. Each morning the irritations would return, but each day they slightly abated. I gradually got used to my traction harness; I learned to move around so that I did not get too fatigued in one position. With the sulfa pills I took every few hours, my fever also lessened.

Although I was improving physically, I had a very negative emotional reaction to what had become my whole wartime experience. The doctors, nurses and hospital staff were all very kind and helpful, but the travail of the past months, and especially the last week, was too much for me. I saw no value or productivity in what I had done, and I felt bemeaned, used, and hurt. Grateful as I was to be alive, I needed something more—some comforting words, or some gesture of recognition and thanks. I felt like crying, but could not manage that either.

I tried to read a little during the day, but my left eye still bothered me. About the third day, I was certain that my eye still had glass in it. So I told a nurse, and she promptly relayed this information to the eye surgeon who had worked on me. That same afternoon the surgeon came in to examine me. He immediately confirmed that I was right. So he put some drops in my eye and skillfully extracted the glass particles that remained. He again bandaged my eye and told me to leave the bandage on for a few days. However, an hour or so later I peeked out from under the bandage to see how it felt. For the first moment since the windshield break, my vision was clear with only a little irritation. Much to my relief, I could read again without discomfort.

My ward-mates were all officers. They were an assortment of different ranks and from many different units. One was an infantry officer—a Major White, who had eight (!) Purple Hearts, meaning one actual Purple Heart Medal and seven Oak Leaf Clusters to go with it. He did not wear them on his uniform, of course. (Nobody did.) Two of his injuries, including the current wound in his stomach, had been serious enough to warrant extended hospitalization.

Gradually as the days passed, the Major recovered to where he could eat and digest solid food. He then gathered together his belongings, but told us all that he had lost his .45-calibre automatic pistol. I knew mine was in my luggage, so I told him he could have it if he wanted it. He was delighted, and arranged to get it from my B-2 bag. I had never done more than examine the weapon briefly when I first got it at Hunter Field in Savannah, so the protective cosmolene was not even cleaned off.

After the Major retrieved the pistol, he cleaned it and filed down the firing pin so that it had a hair trigger. Then, he pressured the hospital's upper echelon officers, who were all doctors, to release him so he could return to his infantry unit—his "old outfit." He seemed to know where it was, and told us all with a chuckle what his commanding officer would say when he saw the Major walk into the command post somewhere near the front lines. He left the hospital just as he wished, and none of us ever saw or heard of him again. Major White was surely a soldier's soldier.

Another Major in the ward, a much younger man who was in the Air Corps, had a broken shin bone (tibia) and was in a "walking cast." When I asked him about his wound, it turned out that he had not been wounded. That frisky horse I had noticed at the Aylesfield House flak shack had kicked him! The slings and arrows of outrageous fortune! He was a humorous and fine person, and shared a laugh at the irony of being "wounded" by a horse while "recuperating" from flak that had missed him.

Another infantryman was a second lieutenant who had been at Bastogne when Von Runstedt's army surrounded the town. A hand grenade fragment had wounded him in the chest. Fine young man. I hope he survived after he left the hospital.

By way of contrast, another lieutenant was a Military Police officer who was in the hospital for hemorrhoid treatment. I learned to dislike him immensely after only a few minutes of conversation. He seemed not to know the difference between a combat soldier and one who was safely out of danger from lethal weapons.

About the second week I was there, orderlies

rolled in a young airman with some broken bones and abrasions, who was the copilot of a B-17 that had cracked up on takeoff. The accident had killed his pilot and some other crew members. Apparently, the pilot had tried to pull the plane off before it was ready to fly. One such mistake was exactly one too many.

My own tenure in the hospital began to stabilize. My physical condition was improving; I could read as much as I wanted; my eating was about normal; I had plenty of people to talk to and no trouble sleeping. Members of my crew dutifully came to visit me, and their presence was therapeutic but brief. Approximately ten days after my last mission with them, they finished their combat tour and could look forward to returning home or to some noncombatant duty. Most of them I never saw again.

These few visits by former crew members were my only contact with the 388th Bomb Group. No higher-ranking officer from any position in my Squadron or Group ever stopped by to see me. I had been with the Group for more than six months, had flown on some of the roughest missions, and had been wounded three times. Surely, some senior pilot or squadron leader, or some adjutant or personnel liaison officer would visit and wish me well. It never happened. The war had become a bore. It was almost over, and everyone was very busy with the finishing details. So, none of them ever visited me in the hospital. Inside me my soul still hurt. I was too young to manage this kind of worldly neglect.

One English civilian came to see me about the third week in February. She expressed her gratitude for the trauma I had endured. Her 'Goodbye' was a particularly melancholy event.

The second day after I was wounded, 30 January 1945, I wrote a V-Mail letter to my parents to reassure them that, though wounded, I was now out of danger. I gave them some details, including the fact that my wound was in my *left* leg, and that my *left* femur was broken. I closed telling them: "The only thing wrong is I'm still a little nauseated from the ether." (I had not actually had any ether, but I did not know that at this point). This letter got to them about a week before the Western Union telegram cited above.

One might ask here: Why would the War Department send a telegram that would not arrive at its destination or be read until long after other means of communication had conveyed the facts in more detail and without all the fuss and fanfare? Just what was the point of the telegram if the news in it was stale and, as here, inaccurate? (I was not wounded in Germany but over Germany.)

The telegram promised "mail address" and "details" from the hospital. Sure enough, the hospital administration sent a form-post card on 30 January. It read:

> "Dear Mr. Timberlake [my father]. . . . :"I am pleased to inform you that on. . . . 30 Jan 1945. . . . your. . . . Son. . . . , 1st Lt. Richard H. Timberlake,. . . . 0-822851. . . . was. . . . Making normal improvement. . . . Diagnosis:. . . . Flak wound and fracture of right [SIC!] leg. . . .
>
> Very truly yours,
>
> W. D. A. G. O. Form 234 Capt. So-and-So,
>
> MAC

Every second week the hospital authorities sent this same form-post card to my parents. Each one mistakenly reported that I was making normal improvement to a "flak wound and fracture of *right* leg." So they never got it right—that is, left. About this time, a letter from my mother puzzled me when in it she referred to the wound in my right leg. I thought *she* could not get it straight. However, 50 years later when I had occasion to examine these post cards closely, I finally understood where the misinformation originated.

The official medical report cited my injury as: "Compound, comminuted fracture of the left femur. Posterior aspect. Wound serious." Even so, most of the bone was still there; the flak had hit no major arteries, and I had full feeling in my leg. My healing system had only to throw calcium across the breaks of the "comminuted" bone, and it would all come together again—I hoped.

At first, my wound was left open to reduce the danger of infection—a normal medical procedure. I did not have any serious pain. It seemed that it would be just a matter of time until the leg would heal. Well, the wound was healing, as the swelling subsided and my fever abated. However, my leg did not yet feel altogether, but continued to feel sort of sketchy and loose. So I was slightly concerned, and wondered when it would feel normal again.

The orthopedic surgeon who had worked on my leg, Major Julian Jacobs from North Carolina, came in to see me regularly. He seemed satisfied with the way the leg was healing, but he would not stay long and talk about it. He was always in a hurry, and no doubt with good reason.

One day, perhaps three weeks after I had been

wounded, Major Jacobs came in again for his routine visit. After his usual observations, however, he put his hands strategically under and over my left thigh and started to bend my leg at the break, up and down, up and down. It was just as though the femur was a piece of malleable metal, and he wanted to see how far it would bend.

I do not remember that his manipulations hurt very much, but they scared me silly. I had no warning, and I could not surmise the purpose of his procedure. After half a minute or so, he stopped, and for once sat down beside my bed. He commented that after he performed this therapy to a patient, he always took a few minutes to visit and show his sympathy. I asked him if he had tried to re-break my leg. He replied that he could not break it, but he could "bend the hell" out of it. He explained further that blood clots in the broken sector were probably interfering with my body's effort to throw out new bone to repair the break. By moving the tissue near the healing pieces of bone, he wanted to break up the blood clots. He left after about five minutes of commiserating, and I was left to wonder how the leg would feel after the shock of his therapy had worn off.

Well, it was a revelation! For the first time since the flak hit it, my leg began to feel as though it was all back together again. It would do what I told it to. I suppose that I might have been more active and diffused the blood clots myself by moving around more than I had. I guess I was afraid to move too much, not knowing how my actions might make things worse. Regardless. The Major's treatment had critically rectified the healing process. From that moment, the bone was ready to grow back to its proper state.

Some peculiar events took place during the two or so months I was in the 65th General Hospital. One night in early March when I was about half-asleep around midnight, I vaguely heard what I thought was a fighter plane approaching at high speed. In the next few seconds, its machine guns started firing—at what I could not imagine. Then, it passed over and lost itself in the night. The next morning we got the news that a German plane had come down low and strafed two villages near Diss, the closest town to the hospital.

The plane was not a fighter, however. It was a Junkers 88 medium bomber; and it did not fire machine guns, but dropped anti-personnel bombs. The attack killed one civilian, injured a few others, and damaged several homes. Apparently, it was a meaningless gesture of some kind or another, just like so much of the war. What the pilot was thinking of, and how and why he would use up scarce German resources to carry out such a senseless sortie, no one could ever know.

Occasionally, the hospital staff held a brief ceremony in the ward to present Purple Hearts to men who had been wounded. If a wound was severe enough, say, a broken bone or worse, the patient would not return to his regular unit. Instead, he would be routed to the "Zone of the Interior," which meant sent back to the United States for further treatment. In such case, he was no longer a part of his former combat unit, so would not get his medal citations as before from his "old outfit." I was one such.

A word is in order on how Army authorities

"awarded" medals. They did not award ordinary medals, such as the Air Medal and Purple Heart, but issued them. All Eighth Air Force flying personnel at this time received an Air Medal for every six missions flown. (I had a total of 26 missions, for example, so I duly received four Air Medals.) Eighth Air Force Headquarters routinely authorized the Medals on a mimeographed form, which was identical for every recipient of the Medal. The common "Citation" read:

> "For meritorious achievement while participating in heavy bombardment missions in the air offensive against the enemy over continental Europe. The courage, coolness, and skill displayed by this Officer upon these occasions reflect great credit upon himself and the Armed Forces of the United States."

The date and order number were typed in at the top, and the recipient officer's name, serial number, rank, group and squadron numbers were typed under the Citation. Finally, official names authorizing the award appeared at the bottom. Some days after an airman had finished a bracket of six missions, he would receive this form in his mail. If he wished, he could then go to the Quartermaster Corps Depot, show the form, and get an actual Air Medal in an attractive case with a blue and gold ribbon.

The sheer number of awards precluded any formal ceremonies. On a given mission that included, say, 1,200 bombers, one-sixth of the personnel active on that mission would be eligible for an Air Medal, or an Oak Leaf Cluster indicating a duplicate award of their existing Air Medal. With nine men on each plane, the average mission qualified 1,800 men for another Air Medal. Assuming the Eighth flew eight bombing missions in an average month, the authorities would issue 14,400 Air Medals (or Oak Leaf Clusters) every month. It was all done "by the numbers."

The Purple Heart was issued much less frequently, but it had a similar mimeographed form. The awarding authority typed in the date and order number, followed by,

> "Subject: 'Awards and Decorations,' the PURPLE HEART is awarded to the following-named Officer [typed in] of the Army Air Forces, United States Army.
>
> "Citation: For wounds received in action against an enemy of the United States on date indicated."

Then, the officer's name, rank, bombing unit, and date on which he was wounded were duly typed in, but nothing about the circumstances of the wound. The Citation did not emphasize his "courage, coolness, and skill," or any other characteristics, as did the Air Medal Citation.

Most of the men I knew did not get the actual medals and Oak Leaf Clusters until they finished their tours and went back to the States. However, very few of my acquaintances had the Purple Heart. Less than one Purple Heart was issued for every fifteen or twenty Air Medals. Very often, the first Purple Heart was also the last, either because it was posthumous or because the wound was bad enough to send the soldier back to the "Zone of the Interior." That would have been my story if my last wound had been my first.

One morning in early February 1945 some nurses and hospital staff gathered in our ward for an awards ceremony. The head nurse read off the names of those patients who were to receive Purple Hearts. She also included my name. However, I already had a Purple Heart, so the order should properly have cited me for an Oak Leaf Cluster to my existing Purple Heart. (Since very few airmen suffered multiple wounds, Eighth Air Force Headquarters may not have had the form for the Oak Leaf Cluster.) I immediately notified the nurse in charge of this mistake.

My correction caused some embarrassment. The Citation had come from Eighth Air Force Headquarters to the 388th Bomb Group, and from the Bomb Group Command to the hospital. Obviously, the personnel administrative unit at the 388th did not know that I had been wounded a second and third times. So they simply forwarded the mimeographed form to the hospital as it came to them.

Hospital authorities now had to handle the matter. They did so by amending the citation with pen-and-ink. Where it read " . . . the PURPLE HEART is awarded . . . ," they penned in a directive arrow, and the words " . . . OLC [Oak Leaf Cluster] to the [PURPLE HEART]." They also penned in the date of my wound, "28 JAN 1945," although the date was already typed in below. In the bottom margin, someone pencilled in "Wd 59 [Ward 59]" and "over." On the reverse of the form, the same pencil had scrawled, "Amended on GO [General Order] #203[.] Extract to be made by your Hq [Headquarters]." The date on the form is 7 February 1945.

Ten days later, 17 February, the amendment appeared as General Order #203. It came to the hospital, where I was now officially stationed, and read in part:

> "So much of General Orders No. 151, as pertains to 1st Lieutenant Richard H. Timberlake, 0-822851, as reads 'Purple Heart,' is amended to read 'Oak Leaf Cluster for wear with the Purple Heart previously awarded'."

The amended Citation was not delivered as a part of any ceremony. It just came with my mail. Now comes the bizarre sequel.

Chapter 15: Further Notes on Awards and a Summing Up

Some decades later, I became curious about the military awards procedures of the World War II era. A news item had surfaced in the 1960s reporting the shameful circumstances under which General Douglas MacArthur had given (not awarded or issued) a Silver Star, the fifth highest U.S. medal, to Lyndon Johnson during World War II. Johnson, who became President of the United States, was a congressman and a Lieutenant Commander in the Navy at the time. One of his assignments had been to visit MacArthur's battle area as a fact-finding investigator for President Roosevelt. When at an Air Force base near Port Moresby, Johnson pressured a combat crew flying B-26s to let him go with them on a bombing mission against a Japanese target on New Guinea.

The mission took place on 9 June 1942 and lasted about three hours. During the mission the B-26 pilots had to take evasive action from Japanese fighters, but otherwise had no casualties and also accomplished nothing of any military value. The tail gunner had managed to shoot down one Japanese plane. When Johnson got back to Port Moresby and reported what had happened, MacArthur told Johnson that he would cite him for the Silver Star, even though no one else on the plane, including the tail gunner, received any award. This one mission was the only combat action in which Johnson participated, and for his part in it he was nothing more than an unwelcome hitchhiker.

The conclusion of Johnson's biographer was that: "Lyndon went home with a 'war record' and a medal [Silver Star] and MacArthur had a new vocal advocate in Washington with some access to the President and more to Congress and the press." In later years MacArthur remarked that if he had known how Johnson was to rise politically, *he would have cited him for the Congessional Medal of Honor!* By this despicable act MacArthur debased the Silver Star into a political bargaining chip, and Johnson willingly cooperated.

The notoriety accompanying this sordid deed prompted many veterans who had seen extended combat during World War II to question just how the military awards system worked. What were official military criteria for awards of the different medals, and what recourse was available for correction of abuses and omissions that had occurred in the past? Most servicemen I talked to knew virtually nothing of awards protocols and procedures. No one I knew who flew with me in England had received even a Distinguished Flying Cross, let alone a Silver Star. So in 1978, when I began to think I might put some of my experiences in writing, I wrote a letter of inquiry to the Military Personnel Records Center in St. Louis for clarification of these questions. After some delay, they directed me to the Air Force Manpower and Personnel Center at Randolph Air Base, Texas.

The Recognition Programs Branch at Randolph emphatically disposed of the notion that the military services might have any specified, objective criteria for awards.

"In order to be considered for an award," my informant wrote, "a written recommendation must have been initiated and placed in military channels within two years of the act, achievement, or service [that occurred] . . . In the absence of a written recommendation, the awarding authority cannot take any action to award a decoration to an individual."

So the answer to my inquiry was, "NO." If no higher officer recommended a serviceman for an award at the time of the incident, the plaintiff could not on his own initiate a review of his case umpty-ump years later no matter how much evidence he had to substantiate it. By the same token, if a high-ranking military authority, such as MacArthur, did recommend an award, the facts of the case could not be an argument against it. It is easy to imagine the many unreported acts of bravery that went unrewarded, as well as contrived "combat" scenarios, such as Johnson's, that resulted in high awards to further some political ploy.

MacArthur could indeed have recommended Johnson for the Congressional Medal of Honor and no one could have stopped him. By comparison with what he could have done, MacArthur's gift of the Silver Star to Johnson was small potatoes—not much more than a political version of the Good Conduct Medal.

The letter from Randolph Field did not end there, however. My correspondent revealed something in the next sentence that I had never known. "Your records do indicate," he wrote, "[that] you were awarded the Purple Heart with *two* oak leaf clusters [my emphasis]."

Two oak leaf clusters? Although I had been wounded three times, two of the three wounds were on my last mission. Therefore, I had always assumed that Air Force Headquarters had compressed my last two wounds together into one Purple Heart. Since I received the one Oak Leaf Cluster only after a headquarters bungle showed that no one knew I had even the first Purple Heart, I could not imagine how or when a second Cluster could have been issued. So I wrote another letter of inquiry asking for the details and circumstances of the second Oak Leaf Cluster.

My respondent replied a few weeks later that the first two Purple Hearts were just as I had them in my records, and the third one—the second Oak Leaf Cluster—was for "wounds incurred in action on . . . 31 January 1945." However, the records contained no further information on how, or where the third wound had happened. Nor could the writer tell me who had issued the Citation, or any other details.

This "Citation" must be a total error. I have no such Citation, and I do not understand how it ever could have existed. On 31 January 1945, I was in skeletal leg traction in a hospital bed, so I could not possibly have been "wounded in action" on that date. I therefore assume that this "ghost" award was made somehow or other on account of my eye wound. Even though that happened on 28 January just before my leg was broken, the opthamalogist did not remove the remaining glass from my eye until 31 January. Still, if hospital officials used my eye wound to grant me another Purple Heart, where is the Citation? Since the Citation does not exist, I do not know what the answer is, and neither I nor anyone else will ever know. Suffice to say, I was wounded three times, and therefore, "by the numbers," should have three Purple Hearts. That is what I have, and there the matter must end. I should emphasize here that, whatever academic interest I may have had in higher awards in an earlier time, I have no such interest now. The facts of the MacArthur-Johnson deceit, coupled with the information from Randolph Field, were enough.

[I eventually got the actual medals, Purple Heart and Air Medal, from a Quartermaster Depot while I was at Billings Army Hospital in Indianapolis. These medals are now in a display case in the Mighty Eighth Air Force Heritage Museum in Pooler, Georgia. The case also contains my pilot wings, the piece of flak that broke my leg, and some photos of me, Major Jacobs, and a very fine nurse (whose name has escaped me) in the 65th General Hospital during March 1945.]

My leg was healing so quickly toward the end of February that Major Jacobs brought some other surgeons in to look at it. They were suitably impressed. I found that I had acquired a reputation for "the quickest broken femur recovery ever recorded."

Part of the reason that my physical recovery

went so well may have been my disposition to "do something" to relieve the tedium of being in bed twenty-four hours a day. As my strength returned, I began experimenting with the traction apparatus that held my leg. I found that I had considerable body movement, except that I could not get out of bed. The ropes attached to my hip-hitch and shin-pin allowed me a fair amount of movement even as they held my leg extended so that the bone would grow back to its normal length. I could pull myself up about four feet completely off the bed so that the orderly or nurse could change the bed under me. In fact, I could hang there indefinitely. And it was no trick at all to put my good right leg down on the mattress and stand on one leg like a crane in a marsh.

I believe that this physical activity accelerated the healing of my leg, especially after Major Jacobs performed his "bend it" therapy on me. I could hardly do myself any harm because the traction apparatus was too well engineered to let me move excessively.

My traction-actions were so unusual that hospital officials had an Army photographer take photos of me "standing up in traction." They sent these photos to my hometown newspaper for publication, but the newspaper never used them. This newspaper's policy was to print photos only of servicemen killed in action. So the hospital administration gave the photos to me. [One of them is in the display case at the Eighth Air Force Heritage Museum in Pooler, Georgia.]

Late in February 1945, doctors took the stitches out of my leg and sewed up the wound. I was now all back together again and ready to be repatriated.

However, to be transported, I had to be put into a plaster cast to prevent my leg from suffering any accidental re-injury. So I was removed from the traction apparatus, Major Jacobs extracted the pin from my shinbone, and hospital orderlies carted me off to the cast shop. There, hospital technicians constructed a cast around my lower half.

The cast came down my right leg to the knee, up to my waist a little above my belt line, and down my left leg to my heel. Between the plaster legs of the cast was a stout wooden spike, which formed a leg of a triangle with the two legs of the cast to make it rigid. Surgeons labeled this contraption a "double hip-spiker" cast. It also had holes in appropriate places. I could now travel.

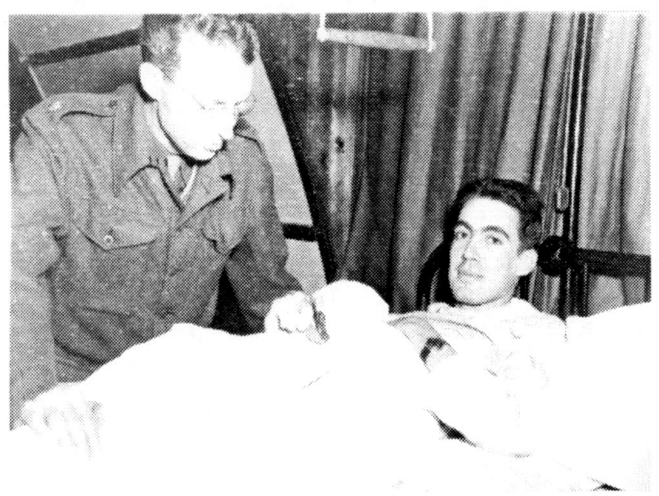

Major Jacobs with the author holding the piece of flak imported from Germany

On 28 March 1945, a hospital ambulance took several other patients and me to a train at Thetford that transported us in turn to Southampton. There, we were loaded onto a U.S. Navy hospital ship to make the sea journey back to the United States. I forget the name of the ship, but it was not very large. I was in the ship's hospital ward and never saw the sea or any other part of the ship except when I was loaded and unloaded. The ship docked in Boston early in April. A train then transported some of us to Billings Army Hospital near Indianapolis, where I recuperated without further incident. By early September 1945, my femur had healed enough so that the medical authorities could discharge me from the hospital and the Armed Forces.

Sometimes all the pieces of an eventful history do not come together until long after the actual occurrences. Such has turned out to be the case for the "mystery" of the missing piece of flak that buried itself in my right leg on August 25, 1944.

As I recounted on page 113 above, the flak piece was not on my bedside table the morning after it was removed from my leg. The surgeon who had operated on me described how difficult it had been to remove the fragments of aircraft aluminum that had piggy-backed into my leg with the flak. However, he was inexplicably vague concerning the whereabouts of the flak itself. Nurses and hospital orderlies suggested that it had been left in the operating room, and that someone there may have disposed of it. Having nothing more to go on, I left it at that.

Fifty-six years after that wartime incident, in

September 2000, I was experiencing some minor pain in my left hip. I advised my orthopedist of this boring fact, so he had some X-rays taken of my hips and pelvic area to see what the problem was. The X-rays showed some slight misalignment of my lower back vertebrae, a common ailment of septuagenarians, and treatable with ordinary medications.

I decided I would like a little more explanation, and asked a radiologist friend of mine to look at the X-rays and explain the problem to me. He kindly assented. So I took the films up to his office and he put them on his viewing screen. One picture showed both my hip joints and the upper sections of both thighs. About two inches below the right hip joint one could also see a very opaque, irregular, and alien object, about the size of a .32-caliber bullet. My radiologist friend, who made his living noticing such things, exclaimed, "Look there. That's a piece of flak!"

Yes, it was. And finally I knew why the surgeon had been so apologetic back there in 1944: he and the other doctors had not removed the flak because they could not find it. It is fairly small—about the size of half a joint of one's little finger. It had penetrated deep into my leg from the side, but at an angle that took it up toward my hip where the surgeon would not expect it. Rather than make more incisions on my leg, which was not seriously damaged, the doctors decided to sew me up and advise me that some of the aluminum "might" still be in my leg. If I had complained later on, they undoubtedly would have tried again to remove it.

The authenticity of the flak is unmistakable. At last I know what happened to it! Since I did not know it was still in my leg, I never had anything done about it. It's there, and it will ever remain there—in the "museum" that is me.

The hospital stays in England and the United States were my last stations in the Army. I never flew again. I had become so obsessed with the trauma and horror of war that I could think only of how such consummate waste and suffering might be prevented. I determined to seek answers by some means or other. This quest became the underlying theme of the professional study I undertook after I left the Air Corps. But that is another story.

This brief account of my flying career, and especially the combat episode, comes, perforce, from one who survived. The events may seem dramatic and adventurous now, but the lad I was then felt anything but daring and confident in that grim fall and winter of 1944-1945. We lived with the dread that our lives on this earth were destined to end before they had fairly begun. Such an unsatisfying and undeserved ending! So, a reader who peruses these pages should not stop with my account. He should imagine to himself what the words would say if written by some of the men who went down.

What, for example, would the men of Bernard Lord's crew have written, if their words could come back to us, after flak and a mid-air collision over Merseburg on 28 September 1944 took most of their lives? Such stories cannot be written; the principals have no means to share their messages. It is left to us who knew and endured to tell something of their suffering, inadequate and incomplete as our descriptions may be. I offer these lines by Stephen Spender as a tribute to those comrades who finished up by going down:

30

Near the snow, near the sun, in the highest fields
See how these names are fêted by the waving grass
And by the streamers of white cloud
And the whispers of wind in the listening sky.
The names of those who in their lives fought for life
Who wore at their hearts the fire's centre.
Born of the sun they travelled a short while towards
the sun,
And left the vivid air signed with their honour.

Stephen Spender, *Poems*, 1934

Richard H. Timberlake Jr.
Bogart, Georgia, 2001

Mission Targets, Dates and Legend, 1944-1945

Mulhouse, France	August 11	Marshaling yard. No flak.
Ludwigshaven	August 14	Synthetic oil plant. Heavy flak.
Zeitz	August 16	Synthetic oil plant. Heavy flak. Sarten lost.
Brux, Czechoslavakia	August 24	Synthetic oil plant. Heavy flak.
Politz, (now part of Poland)	August 25	Synthetic oil plant. Heavy flak. Wounded.
Bohlen	October 7	Synthetic oil plant. German fighters.

Mainz	October 9	Marshaling yard. Light flak.
Cologne	October 17	Marshaling yard. Moderate flak.
Merseburg turnaround	October 30	Seven degrees east. Mission recalled.
Merseburg	November 2	Synthetic oil plant. German rocket planes.
Ludwigshaven	November 5	Marshaling yard. Terrible flak.
Saarbrucken	November 9	Marshaling yard. High clouds. Very cold.
Target Area #2, near Aachen	November 16	Tactical, in support of ground troops.
Lutzkendorf	November 30	Synthetic oil. Heavy, accurate flak.
Mainz	December 4	Marshaling yard. Light flak.
Hanover	December 15	Marshaling yard. Light flak.
Darmstadt	December 24	Airfield. Moderate flak. Largest mission in history of Eighth Air Force.

Koblenz	December 28	Marshaling yard. Light flak.
Kassel	December 30	Marshaling yard. Chaff ship.
Hanau	January 5	Marshaling yard. Light flak.
Ludwigshaven	January 6	Marshaling yard. Moderate flak.
Bischofsheim	January 13	Marshaling yard. Moderate flak.
Augsburg	January 15	Marshaling yard. Light flak.
Rheine	January 20	Marshaling yard. Light flak.
Mannheim	January 21	Marshaling yard. Light, accurate flak.
Hohenbudburg	January 28	Marshaling yard. Moderate very accurate flak. Wounded twice. Landed at base of 100th Bomb Group (Thorpe Abbotts). End of missions. End of tour. End of flying career.